Not A Dead See

Some People and Episodes in the life of
the Diocese of Liverpool
1880-1996

Eric Russell

Foreword by
David Sheppard, the Bishop of Liverpool

Published by:
Eric Russell
16a St. Pauls Street, Southport

First published 1996

British Cataloguing in Publication Data
A catalogue record for this book is available from
the British Library.

Book Production by The Bluecoat Press
Typesetting by Pencilpoint
Printed by The Cromwell Press

ISBN 0 952962 60 8

Preface

In this slight volume I have attempted in a modest way to write an account of the life and growth of the Diocese of Liverpool from the beginning to the present day. I have had to be selective in my choice of persons and events appearing in the story and perhaps some readers will be disappointed to find a person or episode passed over without a mention.

I have tried to set out in an historical sequence those contributions and influences which appear to me to be most significant. I hope the reader will find the book interesting and agree with me at the end of the book that the Diocese is Not a Dead See.

Many thanks are due to Bishop David for writing the Foreword. I am also grateful to Bishop Jim Roxburgh. Canon Alan Bretherton, Canon Owen Eva and Christ Tyne of Church House for kindly reading an earlier draft of the manuscript and offering helpful corrections and improvements. Also to Canon Dick Williams who read the last two chapters and gave me fresh insights into some recent events. I am mindful, too, of many clergy and laity in the Diocese who have generously passed on to me useful information.

The staff of the Local History Departments at Liverpool Central Library and Southport, Crosby, Wigan and St Helens Reference Libraries deserve thanks for their readiness to supply me with relevant material. Also to Headstart History, Publishers, Oxford, for permission to draw on material for the first two chapters from my forthcoming book on *Evangelicalism in the Victorian Church - A Study of Bishop J.C. Ryle, the First Bishop of Liverpool.*

Finally, my appreciation to the following for permission to quote from their publications: Hodder and Stoughton, SPCK, Basil Blackwood, Mowbray, Carnegie Publishing and Reiner Publications.

3.3.2000 / WOMEN'S WORLD DAY OF PRAYER.

"TALITHA KOUM; YOUNG WOMAN STAND UP."

"" STRENGTHEN THOSE WHO HAVE TIRED HANDS
AND ENCOURAGE THOSE WHO HAVE WEAK KNEES"
(ISAIAH 35:3)

Foreword

BY THE BISHOP OF LIVERPOOL
THE RT. REV. DAVID SHEPPARD

Liverpool Diocese has faced great challenges over its 116 years' history. For me the strand that runs through *Not a Dead See* is the Church of England's response to a rapidly-changing urban society.

For many years the demand was to cope with an enormous expansion of population, and the history of building new Churches, developing schools, seeking new forms of ministry, and reaching out in evangelism is an honourable one. More recently the population growth has reversed, employment has declined and we have faced increased deprivation and despair. Eric Russell shows how the Church has sought to share the pain and yet point to a greater hope - symbolised in the magnificent (if protracted) story of the building of the Anglican Cathedral. That is another thread which recurs throughout his story.

Less obvious, but vitally important and constantly recurring, is the move from sectarian conflict between denominations to the authentic co-operation we practice today. I believe there is an old Jewish saying that the last person to appreciate a miracle is the person to whom it happens. This book helps us realise the amazing distance the Merseyside Churches have travelled together in a comparatively short time.

But along the path of these great themes are countless memorable vignettes of individual people, parishes and issues - the real stuff of the life of a Diocese. They bring the story to life. As but one of many examples, I was intrigued to see Bishop Ryle warning of the dangers of clerical dominance in the Church, and of the need to enhance the contribution of the laity. He could have been writing in the mid-1990s!

I congratulate Eric Russell on the result of what appears to have been both hard labour and a labour of love. I hope many will read his book and learn from history why I for one believe there has been no finer place than Liverpool Diocese to meet the challenge of serving Christ in the last 100 years.

Contents

Preface

Foreword
by the Rt. Rev. David Sheppard,
Bishop of Liverpool.

Chapter 1

A New Diocese

The rapid development of Liverpool in the second half of the nineteenth century, due to the increase in trade passing through the Port, led to a phenomenal rise in the population and caught the Church unprepared. There were not sufficient clergy and pastors to minister to the human flood which swept into the town from all parts of the Kingdom in search of work, nor were there the churches and mission halls in the right places to serve the people. It was a situation which challenged the Church and demanded an immediate response.

South-west Lancashire was part of the ancient Diocese of Chester and for a long time it had been felt that the seaport of Liverpool had little in common with the county town of Chester. Commercially Liverpool was far more important, and as a result of the industrial revolution the working classes were being drawn away from the rural areas into the new centres of trade, where there was the possibility of finding work and higher wages.

Earlier in the century, the Bishop of Chester had the oversight of the whole of Cheshire and Lancashire, West Yorkshire and the counties of Cumberland and Westmoreland. In 1836 the Diocese of Ripon was reconstituted and Chester gave up its Yorkshire territory. Another sub-division was made in 1847 when Manchester Diocese was created to provide a better oversight of the religious needs of south-east Lancashire. Chester again lost some of its territory when the counties of Cumberland and Westmoreland were transferred in 1856 to the Diocese of Carlisle. The Diocese of Chester, which in 1541 had been carved out of the huge Diocese of Lichfield, was considerably reduced in size over the years, yet paradoxically, increased in population, because of the growth in trade and industry on the banks of the Mersey.

The first serious proposal to make Liverpool the centre of a new northern Diocese appeared in 1854 in the Report of the Royal Commission on Cathedral Churches, which recommended the creation of additional and smaller dioceses and specifically designated Liverpool as one of them. The Church at the time was unable to implement the recommendation, but the claims of Liverpool and south-west Lancashire to be constituted a separate Diocese were acknowledged in all future debates on the extension of the episcopacy.

Canon Christopher Wordsworth, later Bishop of Lincoln, speaking in the Lower House of Canterbury Convocation in 1859, argued that, since the Church in Australia and New Zealand had bishops to oversee small and scattered congregations, the populous towns of Sheffield, Birmingham and Liverpool had just claims to have their own spiritual leaders.

Several leading churchmen in Liverpool, both clerical and lay, were determined to gain support for the creation of a new Diocese on Merseyside, not only because of the rise in population but also because of the recent establishment of the Roman Catholic Archdiocese. So by means of letters to the press, printed pamphlets, lobbying Members of Parliament and influencing friends in high places, they sought to bring pressure to bear on the Government to introduce a Bill in the House establishing a new See of Liverpool.

The Home Secretary, Richard Assheton Cross, who represented south-west Lancashire in the Commons, was conversant with the strong feelings expressed by Liverpool churchmen, and considered the Liverpool Bishopric, "a feasible and common sense argument".[1] There was a confident hope in the town, that in the near future, he would be able to bring in a Bill leading to the formation of a new Diocese and the appointment of its own Bishop.

The first public meeting to discuss the proposal was convened by John Torr, the Member for Liverpool, in the Town Hall on Friday 8 January 1875. The purpose of the gathering of leading figures in the town, was "to consider the desirableness of seeking a division of the present Diocese of Chester, on the See being vacant, with the object of securing, if practicable, a Bishop for Liverpool".[2] The Archbishop of York had given his general approval to the notion, and the Bishop of Chester, who was closely involved in all the negotiations, had signified his assent to yet a further reduction in the boundaries of his Diocese. After a vigorous debate the meeting unanimously passed three resolutions stating that: it was desirable that Liverpool should be separated from the Diocese of Chester to form the nucleus of an independent Diocese; that the facilities existed for carrying out the scheme of uniting the district with the Isle of Man, and that the union of Sodor and Man with a new Diocese of Liverpool had two distinct advantages: firstly, the scheme would secure a large part of the endowment, and secondly, the end would be achieved without increasing the number of bishops in the northern Province.

The proposed union of Sodor and Man with an English Diocese, a notion first mooted some decades earlier, received a hostile reception from the Manx clergy and press, who saw the proposal as wholly in favour of Liverpool's interests; and for almost a year the clergy of Chester Diocese discussed the scheme, but could reach no agreement. Bishop Jacobson, the Bishop of Chester, might be in agreement with Liverpool becoming a new Diocese, but was opposed to any diversion of endowments, either from Chester or Sodor and Man, to the proposed new See, believing that Lancashire was sufficiently well off to raise the endowment of its own Bishopric. He felt that "the posterity of the men of Lancashire would blush for this generation if recourse were had to any such expedient".[3] Furthermore, a union of Sodor and Man with a new Diocese of Liverpool would be contrary to the present trend and enlarge rather than decrease the size of Dioceses. Faced with such strong opposition, the proposed union, which had appeared so attractive to many churchmen on Merseyside, was quietly abandoned.

Meanwhile, Richard Cross, who had proved himself a wise counsellor of

A NEW DIOCESE

Archbishops, and a sympathetic advocate of episcopal extension, informed the Archbishop of Canterbury that the Government was ready to sponsor a Bill to establish three or four new bishoprics "specifically mentioned". Archbishop Tait consulted those bishops most closely concerned with the division of Dioceses, and no less than nine of them requested consideration. It was difficult to assess the merits of each, and after due consideration, Cross wrote to the Archbishop stating that he was anxious to present the Bill before Parliament to establish several new Bishoprics and had in mind Liverpool, Nottingham, a town in south Yorkshire, Newcastle and Birmingham.

On 1 May 1877, the Home Secretary introduced his Bill in the House to provide the Church with four new Bishoprics, three of them in the Province of York. The machinery for creating the two new Dioceses of St Albans and Truro was already set up, and he hoped that Parliament would readily assent to the new Bill making provision for a limited number of new Dioceses, which he believed would meet the immediate needs of the Church. The Liberationists, a strong Nonconformist body in the House, vociferously opposed the Bill, arguing that there was no demand in the country for more Bishops. The debate was drawn out until it was seen that Cross had left the presentation of the Motion too late in the parliamentary session, and with the pressure of other business, it meant that it had to be withdrawn.

Early in the next session, Earl Beauchamp, the Lord Steward, introduced the first reading of the new Bill in the House of Lords. The debate was maintained at a high level, with strong arguments on both sides, but there was never any doubt that the Lords were in favour of a limited increase of the Episcopate as proposed in the Motion before them. In the Commons, however, it continued to meet with powerful opposition at every stage from the Liberationists, who remembered their success at the end of the last session. Nevertheless, in spite of their rumbustious efforts to talk out the Bill, it reached a third reading and, when a division was called, it was passed by sixty-two votes to twenty. To the delight of many in Liverpool, the new Bishopric Act was approved on 16 August 1878. The four new Bishoprics created by the Act were Liverpool, Newcastle, Southwell and Wakefield.

SEPARATION FROM CHESTER

The Act defined the borders of the new Liverpool Diocese as "the Hundred of West Derby in the county of Lancaster, with the exception of as much of the Hundred as is now in the Diocese of Manchester, and the whole of the ancient parish of Wigan". In addition to the expanding town of Liverpool on the banks of the Mersey, with its densely populated dock areas north and south of the town, the new Diocese included the industrial and mining towns of Wigan and Warrington; chemicals and glass manufacturing in St Helens; the seaside resort of Southport, and the rural districts around Ormskirk and North Meols on the northern boundaries and Childwall and Halewood to the south.

According to the 1871 Census, the population of south-west Lancashire, within the area defined by the Act, was seven hundred and sixty thousand, and in the next ten years it had risen to nearly one million inhabitants, half of whom lived in Liverpool and its environs. Nine Dioceses in England had larger populations, but as J. C. Ryle, the first Bishop, observed: "In none, with the exception of London, is the population per acre so dense and closely packed together as in Liverpool".[4]

The first stage toward creating a new Diocese was now complete, and the next stage was to raise the necessary capital required before the Bishopric could become a reality. Much of the time spent in the parliamentary debates on the Bishopric Bill had centred on the proposed minimum stipend of the bishops and the source of their income. Cross was insistent that Bishops in the newly created Dioceses, should receive an adequate stipend and suggested a minimum of £3,500 per annum. The Bishop of Durham regretted that it was proposed to fix the new episcopal stipends below £4,000, which would deprive these Bishops of opportunities for doing good that were open to their wealthier brethren. Opposing voices felt that such huge stipends were far removed from the poverty of the early Apostles and went some way to explaining why many of the working classes had no time for the Church. Eventually it was agreed that the minimum stipend should be £3,500, with a house up to a rateable value of £500 per annum, rising to a maximum of £4,000 and a house.

While there were some on Merseyside who thought that the time was not propitious to establish a new Bishopric and to raise such a vast sum of money to endow the See; many others felt confident and optimistic that the required sum of £80,000 would be quickly acquired. Firm promises of gifts from £100 to £1,000 had already been given to the Bishopric Committee during recent months, and Cross was able to assure the House, that in the case of Liverpool, he had been informed on good authority that there would be £50,000 in his hands tomorrow, if he wished, as an earnest that the total amount would be reached. The Committee received tremendous encouragement, including donations of £10,000 each from four wealthy citizens in the town,"to start a scheme of securing for Liverpool an independent Bishopric".[5]

For many the dream of twenty years was about to be realised in spite of the economic depression and some public apathy on Merseyside. John Torr was one of the prime movers in the creation of the new Diocese, and for many years he had given himself to its establishment. His sudden death following a stroke was a terrible shock to the people of Liverpool and to his many friends in the House of Commons, and warm tributes were paid him for his magnificent exertions on behalf of Merseyside. The raising of the endowment in so short a time and with little outside help was a remarkable achievement and proof of the enthusiasm of the people of Liverpool and south-west Lancashire to have their own Anglican Bishop.

Chapter 2

FOUNDATION

The population of Liverpool almost doubled between 1861 and 1881 to over five hundred and fifty thousand. In the next twenty years the city had extended its boundaries after adopting the townships of Walton and Wavertree and parts of Toxteth and West Derby, and its population increased to over seven hundred thousand. A large proportion of the inhabitants were Irish immigrants, driven out of their own country by the economic situation, who came to England in search of work and a better way of life. There was also a considerable influx from Wales and Scotland, attracted to Liverpool for the same reasons, in addition to a Chinese community and seafarers of mixed nationalities.

Through the Port of Liverpool, the largest in the United Kingdom at the end of the last century, hundreds of thousands of tons of raw materials were imported, including cotton, grain, meat, sugar-cane, tobacco and timber; and manufactured goods, such as iron, steel, machinery, textiles and pottery, were exported to all parts of the world. The building of the docks and their subsequent extension in 1851, gave employment to thousands of seamen, stevedores, crane drivers, warehousemen, carters and unskilled hands, as well as to bankers, insurance brokers, shipping agents, boat builders, chandlers, and office workers. The railways, and the opening of the Manchester Ship Canal in 1894, a project fiercely opposed by the City Fathers in Liverpool when it was first proposed, were great assets and considerably increased the importance and wealth of Merseyside.

There were lengthy periods of prosperity when the city flourished, but during the occasional slumps in trade the workforce out numbered the jobs available and the ensuing poverty, among the working classes particularly, was appalling. Many of the poorest families at the best of times were condemned to live in underground cellars and dingy, over crowded courtyards, which were always damp and rat infested. Drunkenness, brawling, gambling, immorality and crime were social problems the police found increasingly difficult to deal with.

But there was a brighter side to the city. Liverpool was rich in physical and architectural features, and particularly proud of St George's Hall, built in 1854, and acclaimed as one of the finest classical buildings in the whole of Europe. The town boasted some fine streets of Georgian houses, among them Rodney Street and Catherine Street, and beautiful Abercromby Square. It was not without its generous benefactors, who built the William Brown Library and Museum in 1860, the Walker Art Gallery in 1877, and the Picton Reference Library in 1879; all magnificent buildings on a splendid, rising site in the town centre. And there were many others who gave generously of their money and talents to improve the social, educational and cultural amenities for the good of the people.

FOUNDATION

JOHN CHARLES RYLE

John was the elder son of John Ryle, the Member of Parliament for Macclesfield, a partner in a successful silk mill in the town and co-founder of the Macclesfield and Cheshire Bank. Ryle was a wealthy and prosperous businessman who had great ambitions for his son. He desired a Public School education for him and John was sent to Eton, and from there he won a scholarship to Christ Church, Oxford. He proved himself a brilliant scholar and graduated in 1838 with a First class degree in Classics and Humanities.

It was in his final year at Oxford that he had a remarkable religious experience. He was taken ill sometime before he sat his final examinations, which "brought him very low",[1] and for the first time in many years he began to read his Bible. Sometime later he wandered into a service in an Oxford church and heard someone reading the lesson from Ephesians, chapter 2: "For by grace are ye saved through faith; and that not of yourselves, it is the gift of God". God spoke to him through that Scripture, and in his own words: "I was fairly launched as a Christian".[2] He returned home from Oxford with a First in "Greats", a "Blue" for Cricket and a strong personal faith in Christ.

His father gave him a junior position in the Bank and shortly afterwards he was appointed a magistrate and an officer in the Earl of Chester's Regiment of Yeomanry Cavalry. Once a year his troop was stationed with the Regiment in Liverpool and drilled each day on the sands at Crosby. Ryle had expectations that his son would inherit the business and even enter Parliament, but in the summer of 1841, Daintry and Ryle's Bank suddenly collapsed. The family was bankrupt; lost a fortune of more than half a million pounds, and left their home, Henbury Hall, with only a few private possessions. "We got up one summer's morning with all the world before us", the younger Ryle wrote later in his Memoirs, "and went to bed that evening completely and entirely ruined".[3]

Ryle felt there was only one possible career open to him now, and within months he was ordained by the Bishop of Winchester to a curacy at Exbury. After a couple of years, the Bishop offered him charge of St Thomas', Winchester, a run down church with hardly any congregation, and by his forthright preaching and pastoral ministry, the young rector soon ''filled the church to suffocation".[4] But he was only in the parish a few months before he was invited to move to St Mary's, Helmingham in Suffolk, where he remained rector for seventeen years, till his appointment by the Bishop of Norwich to the living of Stradbroke. Sadly he lost two wives through death at Helmingham, but shortly after moving to his new parish he married Henrietta Clowes, a friend of the family for many years, who became a supportive wife and a caring mother of her new family of five young children.

Ryle soon established a reputation in the Diocese of being a dogmatic and out-spoken Evangelical, a forceful preacher and a prolific writer of gospel tracts. His *Expository Thoughts on the Gospels, Knots Untied, and Holiness*, were volumes widely read, and he became a popular figure at Evangelical Conferences and the annual Church Congresses. He was a man destined for high office and early in 1880 Canon Ryle was appointed Dean designate of Salisbury.

FOUNDATION

When soon afterwards Benjamin Disraeli, the Prime Minister, lost the General Election and he realised that his rival, William Gladstone, the leader of the Liberal Party and a High Churchman, would have the nomination of the first Bishop of Liverpool, he urgently asked Ryle if he would consider going to Liverpool instead of Salisbury? Ryle had reluctantly accepted the Deanery and now he was delighted to be offered the Bishopric of the new Diocese. Disraeli, too, was pleased and relieved that a resolute Evangelical was to have the charge of the new See in Lancashire, since it was created largely through the efforts of Evangelical and Protestant clergy and laymen on Merseyside.

The consecration took place in York Minster on St Barnabas Day, 11 June, 1880, by William Thomson, the Archbishop of York, assisted by three other northern bishops. A longstanding friend of Canon Ryle, Canon William Garbett, preached the sermon before a large congregation of well-wishers, who travelled from Liverpool to York by special trains. The enthronement of the new Bishop took place a few days later in St Peter's pro-Cathedral.

Ryle was sixty-four years of age, six foot four inches in height, broad shouldered, with a long, flowing white beard and in appearance looking every inch a bishop. He had spent most of his ministry in rural parishes, and there were those who felt that he lacked the necessary qualities required to oversee a crowded, industrial Diocese in the north of England. But the Bishop was determined to devote all his energies to establishing a flourishing Diocese on a firm foundation and was confident that he could work amicably with all loyal churchmen to achieve this.

SENIOR APPOINTMENTS

The Venerable J. H. Jones, the octogenarian Archdeacon of Liverpool, continued in office, and to relieve him of some of his duties, Ryle appointed the Rev. J. W. Bardsley, the evangelical vicar of St Saviour's, Falkner Square, as the first Archdeacon of Warrington. When Jones died in 1886, the Bishop transferred Bardsley to Liverpool, and appointed Canon W. Lefroy, a genial Irishman and vicar of St Andrew's, Renshaw Street, in his stead. Lefroy was a pulpit orator and known as "the St Chrysostom of the Evangelical Party". A year later Bardsley was consecrated Bishop of Sodor and Man, and shortly afterwards Lefroy was installed as Dean of Norwich. Bardsley was followed by Canon B. S. Clarke, D.D., vicar of Christ Church, Southport; and Lefroy by Canon W. F. Taylor, D.D., incumbent of St Chrysostom's, Everton, a militant Protestant and leader of the Orange Order in Liverpool. When Archdeacon Clarke died in 1895, Ryle transferred Dr Taylor to the Archdeaconry of Liverpool and appointed Canon T. J. Madden, vicar of St Luke's, Bold Street, to the Archdeaconry of Warrington.

The Bishop had the gift of twenty-four canonries and he selected fifteen to begin with from among the Evangelical and Broad Church clergy in the Diocese, but Anglo-Catholics were not included. Within a few years he filled the remaining vacancies with carefully chosen men.

7

FOUNDATION

THE DIOCESAN CONFERENCE

Ryle was an eloquent platform speaker and an accomplished debater, having been schooled in the art at the Church Congresses, so he had no fear of chairing large annual conferences. The first Diocesan Conference met in St George's Hall in the autumn of 1881 and called together all the Diocesan clergy and elected lay representatives for two days discussion of Diocesan business. Ryle believed that "a bishop was never meant to be a mere figure head",[5] and he took the opportunity in his Presidential addresses of airing his views and exhorting the clergy to fulfil their ministry. His opinions did not always meet with approval, and whenever he was defeated in a vote he would remind Conference that he was "a big man getting on for sixteen stone and he could not help treading on peoples' toes".[6]

It was customary for the Bishop to hold a Triennial Visitation, at which he met with clergy and laity to survey the work of the Diocese and express his hopes for the future. Usually the Bishop's Charge was delivered in St Peter's pro-Cathedral and the parish church of another town the following day. Each of Ryle's addresses lasted at least ninety minutes and were "plain spoken, straight-forward" statements on the pressing needs of the Diocese such as the need for more clergy, more church buildings, and more schools and mission halls. With good humour, Ryle admitted that "when a bishop has passed the stage of three score years and ten he is bound to remember that each Triennial Visitation may be his last - so he leaves nothing unsaid".[7]

PLANS FOR A NEW CATHEDRAL

In his Primary Visitation Charge, given in a crowded pro-Cathedral, Ryle spoke of "the want of a Cathedral in Liverpool worthy of such a great city". The Bishopric Act had designated St Peter's as the Cathedral Church of the new See, but many churchmen believed that a new Diocese should have a new Cathedral built to the glory of God, which could be of use for the benefit of the whole Diocese.

A Cathedral Committee was appointed and given the task of finding a suitable site in the city. In all, twenty-three were considered, among them St Peter's in Church Street, St James's Mount, and St John's Churchyard. After many meetings and months of discussions, no agreement could be reached and interest in the project gradually waned. But eventually the Committee did settle on the St John's site behind St George's Hall, and application was made to Parliament to create the Liverpool Cathedral Act, which was passed on 25 June 1885.

Several architects were invited to submit plans, and the design of William Emerson, a distinguished Church architect, was accepted by the Committee. But no sooner was it agreed upon than several members had second thoughts about the suitability of the architect's plans in relation to the chosen site. It was felt that a Gothic style church as proposed by Emerson, surmounted by a huge dome, would be too great a contrast so close to the classical lines of St George's Hall. So Emerson was asked to submit another plan in a second competition, but he brusquely refused, saying that it was unfair, "to ask the winner of a race to compete the second time because the committee chose to change the shape of the Cup".[8]

The problem remained unresolved, and eventually the Cathedral Act lapsed and the project was left in abeyance until a more opportune time. It was a genuine disappointment to the Bishop, to Sir William Forwood, the treasurer and the majority of church people in the Diocese. But with hindsight it is evident that the deferment was for the best.

CHURCH ATTENDANCES

In October 1881, the *Liverpool Daily Post* aroused great interest among its readers by publishing the results of a religious survey in the city. On Sunday morning, 16 October, representatives of the newspaper attended the main services in all the churches and chapels to count the number of sittings available and the attendances. The survey revealed that the Church of England provided sittings for seventy-five thousand people and the average attendance was three hundred and nine worshippers. St Chrysostom's, Everton, was the best attended, with a congregation of one thousand.

Ryle was disappointed with the findings of the Census, though not surprised. However, some Nonconformists complained that a morning count favoured the Church of England, and suggested there should be a Census taken on a Sunday evening. *The Liverpool Daily Post* obliged, and the results of the count taken on Sunday evening, 6 November, showed that all denominations had larger congregations in the evening, with the exception of the Roman Catholics and Presbyterians. Three Anglican congregations topped one thousand worshippers; St Andrew's, Renshaw Street, St Augustine's, Shaw Street and St Nathaniel's, Windsor, where the Bishop happened to be the preacher.

Canon A. Hume, the incumbent of All Soul's, Vauxhall, a sociologist, questioned the accuracy of the survey and persuaded the Diocesan Conference to authorise a credal survey throughout the Diocese, believing that it would produce a truer picture of the strength of the Church of England in south-west Lancashire. Each parish appointed numerators to visit every home to ascertain the size of the family and its religious affiliations. The published results showed that the Anglican Church had the allegiance of 56% of the population, the Roman Catholics 24% and the Noncomformists 19%.

The Bishop accepted Hume's report and concluded that the difference between affiliation and attendance was due to two weaknesses: generally poor preaching in the pulpit, and the lack of pastoral visiting. Amend these and, he believed, attendances in the Church of England would improve.

To satisfy himself about the real state of Church attendances, Ryle arranged for a census to be conducted on Trinity Sunday, 1882. Clergy were notified beforehand in confidence and warned not to pressure anyone to attend services. The weather was inclement, which may have affected attendances, nevertheless, it was recorded that one hundred and sixty-five thousand attended churches and mission-halls during the day. No note was made of worshippers attending more than once and probably some attended as many as three services. Significantly, results showed that numbers were slightly lower than those recorded the previous autumn.

The *Daily Post* repeated the religious survey in October 1891 and again in 1902, and it was observed that some churches were not fairing so well. At St Chrysostom's, Everton the congregation in 1891, had dropped to four hundred and fifty at the morning service and at St Andrew's, Renshaw Street. it had fallen to two hundred and forty. On the other hand, attendances at St Augustine's, Shaw Street, rose from four hundred and sixty-seven to one thousand and forty, with thirteen hundred and thirty-six worshippers at the evening service.

MORE CLERGY

Ryle firmly believed that the mission of the Church was to preach the gospel, to administer the sacraments and to strengthen believers in the Faith. He considered the parochial system an ideal situation for fulfiling this aim, and in his Primary Charge he emphasised the point, saying: "If the Established Church in this country claims to be the Church of the people it is her bounden duty to see that no part of the people are left like sheep without a shepherd". However, for this task more men were urgently required to serve in the parishes.

He was a founder member of Wycliffe Hall, Oxford, a theological college opened in 1877, and also on occasions a Select Preacher at the University, and through these and other contacts he did everything in his power to attract evangelical ordinands to his Diocese. Generally, it happened that there were slightly more Cambridge than Oxford graduates serving in the Diocese, since Cambridge among its students had a more evangelical tradition. In addition, the Diocese attracted several men from Durham and St Aidan's Theological College, Birkenhead.

After completing their course at University or Theological College, ordinands were required to sit the Bishop's own Deacons' and Priests' examinations, and it appears that not all candidates were accepted. Early on in the Episcopate three men hoping to take Priests' Orders were rejected because of "utter ignorance and inefficiency", and two Deacons for "unsoundness in doctrine". Ordinations took place on Trinity Sunday and at Advent in the pro-Cathedral, and three days before the service, candidates attended at the Bishop's Palace for interviews. Each evening after supper, the Bishop spoke to the ordinands from an open Bible, and always instructed them, "Read your Bible, young men, Read your Bible".[9]

Once a year the Bishop invited all those he had ordained to a gathering at St Nathaniel's, Windsor. With good humour the annual meetings soon became known among the younger clergy as "The Bishop's Priests' Parties". The day began with Holy Communion conducted by the Bishop, assisted by Canon Hobson, the incumbent. After the service the clergy adjourned to Windsor Mission Hall nearby for the first address of the day, given by a well-known evangelical speaker on some aspect of the minister's life and work.

In many downtown parishes there was no suitable housing for the clergy and the Bishop gave permission for these to live outside their parishes. No less than seven clergy families lived on Richmond Terrace, Anfield Road. Such clergy were affectionately known among Liverpudlians, who saw them travelling daily between their homes and churches, as "the tram-car clergy".

Ryle made every effort to raise the stipends of his clergy, which in some instances were appallingly low. Following a Diocesan report on clergy income, Ryle set up a Sustentation Fund in 1891 with a capital of £1,000, which aimed to provide clergy in parishes of less than five thousand parishioners with a stipend of £200 per annum, and those in larger parishes with a minimum of £235 per annum. The Diocese did have the distinction of being the first, after the Archdiocese of York, of establishing a Diocesan Incumbents Pension Fund in 1891 with a capital of £1,000, which enabled sick and aged clergy to retire on a small pension.

The creation of new Dioceses often led to an increase in the number of ordinations. In the decade prior to the formation of the new Diocese, Bishop Jacobson ordained one hundred and eighty-eight deacons and in the next decade Bishop Ryle ordained two hundred and ninety-eight and, in all, a total of five hundred and fifty-three deacons. In addition, he ordained no less than five hundred and forty-one priests to serve in the Diocese.

USE THE LAITY

The Bishop was concerned that the laity, many of whom he believed possessed great gifts, had little say in Church affairs and were rarely consulted on matters of policy. He was a reformer ahead of his time and advocated that the laity should have a voice in Convocation, in Diocesan affairs and be more engaged in the work of the parishes. He believed no incumbent should attempt to run his parish without constantly consulting the laity. He insisted that "a mischievous habit of leaving all religion to the parson has overspread the country",[10] at a time when the laity should be making an active contribution to the work and growth of the local church. Consequently he believed the Church was losing ground in the parishes because the clergy were failing to involve lay people sufficiently by encouraging them to use their many gifts.

Through Ryle's leadership the Diocese established the Lay Helpers Association and the Scripture Readers Society, which offered enrolled members the opportunity of house to house visiting, sick visiting, tract distribution, and assisting in mission services alongside the clergy in poor parishes. Hundreds of dedicated laity willingly gave their time and talents to serving Christ in this way. Mrs Ryle, too, was an enthusiastic supporter of the Liverpool Ladies' Parochial Bible and Domestic Mission, which did a similar work with women helpers.

MORE CHURCHES

The Church Census returns revealed that some churches were losing their congregations, yet it was known that there were other parishes where there was a growing population without adequate church buildings. In the course of his first Visitation Charge, Ryle briefly reviewed the history of the Church in south-west Lancashire and stated that in 1687 there were only twenty-five churches in the area covered by the Diocese. Thirteen more churches were consecrated between 1794 and 1826. But since that date one hundred and twenty-five churches had been built and consecrated. The period between the 1820s and the 1880s was a boom period in Anglican church building. In his address, Ryle proposed that the Diocese set up *A Twelve Churches Fund*, and asked the wealthy citizens of Liverpool to give generously to meet this need through the Diocesan Church Building Society. There was a fair response to the appeal and by 1884, the Secretary of the Society confirmed that eighteen new churches were in process of erection at an average cost of £7,000, for the site, building and endowment. Eighteen months later he reported to the Diocesan Conference that twelve new churches had been consecrated; four had been licensed and were awaiting endowment and repair funds, and four more were in course of erection and would be completed the following year.

Reviewing the work of the Diocese in 1887, the Bishop reported on the achievements of the various agencies, and observed with some pride that there were now two hundred incumbents and one hundred and fifty-four assistant clergy serving in the Diocese. Since its foundation twenty new churches had been consecrated, two licensed, and many more were being renovated and restored. In addition, there were fifty licensed mission halls, three of them in the charge of missionary curates.

Many churches in the Diocese, such as St Bride's, Toxteth, were built of brick and had no special architectural features, while others were commissioned by private patrons like Douglas Horsfield, who engaged J. L, Pearson, a celebrated church architect, to draw up plans and design the interior of St Agnes', Toxteth. The church is a fine example of Victorian ecclesiastical architecture with its stone groined ceiling, the chancel pavement laid with various coloured marble, and the reredos, pulpit and font all carved of alabaster. In contrast, in those poorer parishes, where it was necessary to provide additional accommodation and money was not available to build a splendid new church, the church day school might fill a gap or even "a tin tabernacle" might be erected. These iron churches were manufactured locally by Isaac Dixon at his Windsor Iron Works, and according to an advertisement, they were "tasteful in design, economical, durable, made of the best materials, and erected in the most careful manner".[11] St Benedict's, Everton, started as an iron church, when the parish was carved out of St George's in 1878, and was in constant use until "a proper church" was opened some years later.

Most churches in Victorian times, unless they had a large endowment, relied for funds partly on the Sunday collections and the paid pew system. Among the churches built in Ryle's day, only a small number, including St Dunstan's, Edge Hill, and St Simon's, Anfield, were free and unappropriated; while St Bede's, Toxteth, was one that could afford to leave only half the sittings free. A paid pew usually cost between 10/- and £1 per annum. Ryle was not happy with the system, recognising that it was really a hindrance to the work of the Church and offered an excuse to families, on low wages or none at all, not to attend. The practice gradually fell into decline, but it was not until much later in the next century that it was finally abolished.

Ryle was a great builder of churches and during his tenure of office forty-two new churches were consecrated and forty-eight mission halls built and licensed.

FOUNDATION

RITUAL CONTROVERSY

The Catholic Revival in the Anglican Church, which began in Oxford in the 1830s, developed in the 1850s onward an elaborate ceremonial in worship, through the use of art, music and Gothic architecture. Soon among Anglican priests there emerged a new generation of "Ritualists", who claimed to restore to the Church of England some of the ceremonial discarded at the Reformation.

In 1881 there were only five Anglo-Catholic churches within the Borough of Liverpool, and the number in the Diocese did not increase substantially during Ryle's Episcopate. It was known that he was "obnoxious to all High Churchmen",[12] and Ritualists had no real desire to work in his Diocese.

Because of his known Protestant views, it was no surprise when not long after arriving in the Diocese, Ryle became involved in one of the most celebrated prosecutions in the Victorian Church. The dispute between the Bishop and the Rev. James Bell-Cox, the perpetual curate of St Margaret's, Princes Road, Liverpool, began when Ryle's attention was drawn to a report in the *Liverpool Courier*, describing a service at St Margaret's, at which lighted candles were on the altar, incense was used and the priest wore a cope and biretta. It was generally understood that these practices contravened the so-called *Ornaments Rubric in The Book of Common Prayer* as well as the Public Regulation Act of 1874. The Bishop felt obliged to talk privately with Bell-Cox and appeal to him to modify his ceremonial, but he did so without success, and the ritual continued uninterrupted.

Speaking sometime later in the Upper House of Convocation at York, on the subject of the *Ornaments Rubric*, Ryle said that he had met with some ritualistic problems in his Diocese, but he had no intention of prosecuting any of his clergy since he believed it would do more harm than good.

However, when it became evident that the Bishop was not prepared to discipline one of his recalcitrant clergy, the matter was taken up by James Hakes, a Liverpool consultant and chairman of the local branch of the Church Association. The Association was established in 1865 to maintain the Protestant and Reformed character of the Church of England. Early in 1885 Hakes complained to the Bishop that no less than thirteen illegal ceremonial acts had taken place in a service conducted by Bell-Cox at St Margaret's, and he threatened to institute proceedings in the Ecclesiastical Court if Ryle did not curtail the offending ritualism.

Again Ryle appealed to the priest to conform for the sake of peace within the Church, and warned that unless he obeyed, he had no alternative but to allow litigation to go forward. Bishops had the right of veto in such cases, but Ryle refused to exercise the option believing that it deprived a citizen of the right of justice. When it became known in the Diocese that Bell-Cox was to be prosecuted, petitions to halt the lawsuit from both the clergy and the laity were presented to the Bishop, but the case went ahead.

Twice the offending priest was summoned to appear before Lord Penzance, Judge of the Chancery Court of York, and twice he failed to appear. On the second occasion he was suspended from office for a period of six months, but he ignored the injunction and continued to take the services at St Margaret's with the usual ritual.

13

FOUNDATION

On 5 May 1887, the Judge sentenced Bell-Cox in his absence to a period of imprisonment for "manifest contumacy and contempt of court".[13] He was arrested just as he was about to enter his church to conduct the daily Mass and taken to Walton Jail. The Bishop was clearly upset by the turn of events and instructed Archdeacon Bardsley to try every avenue to secure the clergyman's release.

Fortunately for Bell-Cox, his legal counsel discovered a technical peculiarity in the Court's proceedings and the Judge ordered an immediate discharge of the prisoner. Bell-Cox spent sixteen days in prison and on his release returned to St Margaret's to a hero's welcome. Hakes was disappointed at the outcome, but did not give up and took the case to the Court of Appeal, which reversed the Judgment. Then Bell-Cox appealed finally to the House of Lords, where eventually Judgment was given in his favour.

RELATIONS WITH OTHER CHURCHES

Ryle believed that the Church of England, being a National Church, must embrace men of different opinions, in the same way that a nation's army includes various regiments. So when he was consecrated a Bishop he was determined to work amicably with men of High, Broad and Low Church traditions, who were faithful and loyal to the Church's formularies. He recognised the importance of Christian unity and it was his constant aim to work for closer relations between the clergy in the Diocese. He saw that the want of unity perplexed the laity, kept young men out of the ministry, weakened the Church's witness and hindered the work of evangelism.

He never forgot his family connections with Nonconformity, and was delighted, when on his arrival in Liverpool, the Methodists presented him with a copy of the Bible and *The Methodist Book of Praise*. It was the beginning of a long and friendly association. He was always ready to support their causes and it led to him becoming known as "The Nonconformist Bishop of Liverpool". On the occasions when the Methodist Conference was held in the city, he invited the President and other Methodist guests to the Palace, and expressed his good wishes and prayers for the success of their Conference.

The abolition of the Church Rate in 1868, the removal of religious tests in 1871, which opened Oxford, Cambridge and Durham Universities to Dissenters, and a change in the law in 1880 permitting Nonconformists to officiate at burials in Church graveyards, all helped to remove some of the grievances against the privileges of the Established Church.

Relations with Roman Catholics were not so close. There is no evidence that the Bishop fostered any rapport with Archbishop Bernard O'Reilly or his successor Archbishop Thomas Whiteside. In practical terms the numerical strength of the Roman Catholic allegiance in Liverpool, and in the rest of the Diocese raised many problems. The majority of Irish Catholics who landed in Liverpool looking for work belonged to the lower classes and most of them gravitated to the lower parts of the city around the docks, or settled in the poorer quarters of nearby towns. They tended to have large families and whole neighbourhoods soon took on a predominantly Protestant or Catholic character.

FOUNDATION

Early in his Episcopate, the Bishop and his family were attacked in their carriage by a mob of Irish Roman Catholics as they were leaving St Michael-in-the-Hamlet. Missiles were thrown, but no one was hurt and the damage was superficial. Generally the sound of a band leading a Protestant or Catholic procession was an invitation to the "Opposition" to stand and jeer and, all too often, this developed into violence and numerous arrests by the police.

The two denominations, Anglican and Roman Catholic, were far apart and went their separate ways. Ryle had made his position clear long before he became a Bishop and he never changed his stance: "When Rome has repealed the decrees of Trent, and her additions to the Creed; when Rome has recanted her false and unscriptural doctrines; when Rome has renounced image-worship, Mary worship and transubstantiation, then, and not till then, it will be time to talk of reunion with her".[14] It was a view generally held within the Diocese.

THE CHURCH AND THE POOR

The Victorian Church and contemporary society were deeply class conscious and when Ryle came to Liverpool he saw the raw divisions caused by extreme wealth and extreme poverty. He did not believe that the Church had any easy solutions to meet the social problems of the day, except to urge the down-and-outs to try and improve their lot by means of self-reliance and persistent exertions, as well as encouraging the clergy to support all the legislative measures which promoted temperance, purity, thrift and helped to provide healthy dwellings.

He was not a champion of the poor, but in the Diocese he gave his whole-hearted support to the Sunday School Movement, Church Day Schools, the Band of Hope, the Diocesan Board of the Temperance Society, the Diocesan Waifs and Strays Society, the Mersey Mission to Seamen and the Liverpool Seamens' Orphan Institute.

Ryle was a strong advocate of the temperance movement and recognised "the Demon Drink" to be the root cause of so much misery and poverty. The Temperance Society in Liverpool was the largest and most vigorous branch outside London. The work included the Police Court and Prison Gate Mission, the Firewood Factory at Bootle, the Penny Bank and the Sick and Benefits Society. In 1898 the Society provided seven thousand breakfasts for released prisoners from Kirkdale Prison, one thousand pledges were made, and one hundred and sixty-two men were given jobs at the Firewood Factory. The Society campaigned passionately to curb the number of licences granted by the Corporation to corner-shops for the sale of beer and stout, which encouraged intemperance among women, children and servants.

The Bishop and his family were regular worshippers at St Nathaniel's, Windsor, where many working class families attended. He did not believe that the poor were lost to the Church, but that they needed sympathy, loving support and a clear presentation of the Gospel. At one Congress meeting, he described St Nathaniel's as "a parish of five thousand people with not a rich man in it, but only small shop-keepers, artisans and poor....There are one hundred and thirty-three families living in cellars".[15] He said that the ministry began in a cellar, by the incumbent, Canon Richard Hobson, before the church was built, and went on to say that, on one occasion at a Communion Service, when he distributed the consecrated elements to the communicants, he "saw the hands which received them and I knew that many of them were dock labourers and foundry men".[16] It was his firm conviction that the evangelical faith and no other could show positive results of changed lives in the great semi-heathen parishes in colliery districts and manufacturing towns.

PETER SORENSON ROYSTON

In 1891 Ryle suffered a slight stroke from which he made a remarkable recovery, but it became obvious that if he was to avoid a complete breakdown he needed to share his episcopal duties. Bishop Royston had recently returned to England after serving for thirty-five years in the Colonies with the Church Missionary Society; nineteen of them as Bishop of Mauritius. The Victorian Church made good use of its missionary bishops when they returned home and Ryle was delighted to appoint Royston, his Assistant Bishop. Ryle was now seventy-five years of age and he found Royston an invaluable help in relieving him of some of his preaching engagements, inductions and confirmations. Ryle described him as "a dear and saintly man", and Royston frequently recalled in later life the weekly staff meetings at the Bishop's Palace, which always concluded with "the two bishop's kneeling together and commending themselves, their ministry and the Diocese to the Lord".[17]

THE CLOSING YEARS

In 1896 Ryle celebrated his eightieth birthday and to mark the occasion Archdeacon Taylor and other representatives of the Diocese, including the Rev. James Bell-Cox, presented him with an illuminated Address at the Bishop's Palace. The Bishop was overcome by the affectionate tones of the Address and was only saddened that Mrs Ryle could not share the joy with him.

It was while attending the great Liverpool Exhibition in 1886, on the occasion of Queen Victoria's visit to the city, that she caught a chill from which she never fully recovered. She died on 6 April 1889 and was buried in Childwall Churchyard. Between five and six thousand mourners stood outside the Bishop's Palace to witness the cortege leave, and many travelled to Childwall to pay their respects. The Bishop felt the loss grievously and was marvellously sustained by his daughter, Jessie Isabella, and occasional visits by Herbert, his son, with his family.

In 1894, as part of the Diocesan initiative to stem the tide of indifference among the working classes to the Christian message, the Bishop sponsored the Liverpool General Christian Mission, led by the Rev. W. Hay Aitken and Prebendary W. E. Askwith, with supporting missioners. A decade earlier, Ryle had welcomed the American evangelists, Sankey and Moody, to Liverpool and sat on the platform in Hengler's Circus, when Moody preached to a congregation of five thousand and many confessed faith in Christ in response to the gospel message.

The Bishop paid tribute to Moody's ministry at York Convocation, but he was an advocate of the parochial system in the Church of England, believing that the regular evangelistic and pastoral ministry of a man of God in the parish is the most effective way of evangelism. He wrote a Pastoral Letter asking parishioners to pray for the

Mission, to attend regularly, and to invite others to go along. "The benefits of the Mission", he wrote, "do not consist in temporary excitement and running after strange preachers, but in the new sense of the value of souls, leading to repentance, faith, and practical holiness. It is only when the Bible is read, Sunday kept better, the Lord's Table better attended, that the Mission does any real good". Most parishes in the Diocese took part in the Mission, and at the final Thanksgiving Service in the pro-Cathedral, many clergy testified that their churches had been filled, people converted and church members revived.

Throughout his ministry Ryle had been an enthusiastic supporter of Home and Overseas Missions. He was a Vice-President of the Church Missionary Society and often spoke at their Annual Meetings in London and elsewhere. In 1896 he addressed the Missionary Conference in Liverpool organised by the Student Volunteer Missionary Movement, and urged the large audience of young people to go out and evangelise the world in that generation. The Bishop's last sermon was preached on behalf of CMS at St Silas' Church, Toxteth Park, where his friend, Canon W. H. Woodward, was the vicar. In the course of his address he told the congregation that he had just received a postal order for 23/- from a nurse, who wished the money to go to missionary work. At the close of the service, when the offering was taken up, it was discovered that someone had placed a gold chain in one of the collecting plates, in response to the Bishop's challenging appeal.

In November 1899 Ryle notified the Archbishop of York that he intended to retire from the Bishopric at the end of February 1900. For some months he had been in poor health and he realised that he must make room for a younger and more energetic lead-er in the Diocese. He attended St Nathaniel's church for the last time on Christmas morning, accompanied by his son and daughter, and received Communion from Canon Hobson. At their farewell meeting in the Palace he presented his friend with one of his treasured study Bibles, and said, "Now let us have a parting prayer. I knelt by his chair", Hobson recalls, "and oh, what a prayer he offered for me! I shall never forget it".[18]

The Bishop retired with his daughter to their new home in Lowestoft, a resort he loved so much. But only eleven weeks after leaving Liverpool, and just one day short of the twentieth anniversary of his consecration, he died. He was buried beside his wife in Childwall Churchyard and his memorial stone bears his favourite text: "By grace are ye saved through faith..." (Eph. 2.8).

Under Bishop Ryle's leadership the Diocese created a lively Diocesan Conference, built many new churches and mission halls, increased the number of clergy and raised clergy stipends. Many churches were open for daily prayer, and Holy Communion was offered in every parish church at least once a month. Plans for a new Cathedral did not materialise, but Church House became his memorial in stone, and from that base several Diocesan Institutions advanced the evangelistic and social aspects of Church's mission. It was widely acknowledged that during his Episcopate, Ryle had established a strong Evangelical Diocese on a firm foundation.

Chapter 3

CONSOLIDATION

The twentieth century began in an optimistic mood with bright hopes for the future. Tremendous changes had taken place during the closing decades of Queen Victoria's reign. The State now provided free elementary education for all children up to the age of twelve years, automobiles began to replace the horse-drawn carriages of the rich and electric tramcars were a new novelty. Department stores were expanding in the town centres and there was a gradual improvement in housing, living standards and public health.

Only the War in South Africa cast its shadow over a bright future. The newspapers were full of reports of the fighting and every day there were long lists of the killed and wounded. However, the relief of the garrisons at Ladysmith and Mafeking were expected and there would be great rejoicing when the troops returned home.

Liverpool had already entered the twentieth century with its Overhead Railway along the length of the docks, the first overhead railway in Europe. The Port was the gateway to the Empire and larger, faster steam ships, carrying passengers and goods, were replacing the old square riggers.

Ecclesiastically, the Diocese was well established with a strong evangelical hue, with many thriving churches and a people quietly awaiting the appointment of the new Bishop and a new era in the life of Church on Merseyside.

FRANCIS JAMES CHAVASSE

Rumours and speculations are always rife when the name of a new bishop is to be announced. Among several names it was strongly rumoured that Charles Henry Turner, the Sufragan Bishop of Stepney, might be appointed, but no one had suggested the name of Chavasse and it came as a complete surprise when the Principal of Wycliffe Hall, Oxford, was nominated. He had spent most of his ministry among "the dreamy spires of Oxford" and was hardly known in Liverpool.

Chavasse loved his work in Oxford and an invitation from Lord Salisbury, the Prime Minister, inviting him to be the next Bishop of Liverpool was a surprise to him also. Some years earlier, the Bishop of Exeter, Edward Bickersteth, had invited him to be his Suffragan Bishop of Crediton, but he felt he could not leave Wycliffe, and besides, he believed there were far better qualified men for the position and graciously declined the offer. Now he was again faced with a difficult decision. Should he stay in Oxford and train future bishops or become one himself? Friends urged him to accept the challenge of strengthening the foundations laid by Ryle at Liverpool. So somewhat reluctantly, he replied to the Prime Minister, and "with a heavy heart and with many misgivings",[1] he allowed his name to go forward, yet with the firm conviction that "if God bids, he enables".[2]

CONSOLIDATION

For more than twenty years, he had exercised an evangelical ministry in a city dominated by Tractarian teaching. As Principal of Wycliffe Hall and Rector of St Peter-le-Bailey, he had quietly followed a pastoral and teaching ministry among students and parishioners. In this niche he expected to spend many more years. His preaching attracted large congregations, so much so that his friend, Canon Christopher, in the neighbouring parish of St Aldate' s pleaded with him in jovial terms: "Don't enlarge your church, brother, or I shall have no congregation left".[3]

Meeting Chavasse for the first time left everyone struck by his diminutive size; he was only five foot three inches tall. Unfortunately, when he was still a schoolboy, he suffered a bout of measles, which led to complications, resulting in a serious curvature of the spine from which he never recovered. Though small in stature and delicate in health, he was great in heart, with a sure personal faith solid as a rock.

He was consecrated Bishop of Liverpool in York Minster by Archbishop Maclagan, assisted by fourteen bishops, on St Mark's Day, 25 April, 1900. Usually the consecration of bishops took place in the Quire of the Minster, but on this occasion, because of the large numbers expected to attend the Consecration, the Nave was used for the first time and it was filled to overflowing with friends and well-wishers from all parts of the country. The sermon was preached by his friend, Dr. Handley Moule, The Norris Professor of Divinity at Cambridge, who only a year later was himself consecrated in the Minister to be Bishop of Durham.

The Enthronement of the new Bishop took place in St Peter's pro-Cathedral the following Thursday in the presence of the Lord Mayor and Corporation and representatives of the clergy and laity, followed by lunch in the Town Hall. The Diocese gave him and Mrs Chavasse a warm and generous welcome and afterwards, the Bishop paid a glowing tribute to J. C. Ryle, his predecessor, and expressed his hopes for Liverpool and the Diocese in the future. *The Church Review* said of him: " There was no reason to be dissatisfied with the selection that has been made....a Low Churchman was a necessary choice considering the tradition of the See, and the recent political agitation, though a bitter disappointment to the Orange Order". Another publication, *Church Bells*, described Chavasse as a leading Evangelical of great influence in the Church, untainted by party-spirit, and went on to say: "The Diocese has gained a bishop of high spiritual character and possessed of great pulpit power". The *Church Times* was also generous in its welcome, stating that: "Unless the fulfilment belies the promise the Episcopate should be marked by a quickening of church life".

A man of deep and sincere faith, Chavasse came to the Diocese relying entirely on the grace and power of God and not on any abilities of his own. He became a familiar figure in the busy streets of Liverpool. This small man, dressed in episcopal garb, with top hat, gaiters and buckle shoes, was instantly recognised. He had no wish, however, to be the "the Lord Bishop", but rather "a Father in God" among his people and it was not unknown for him to help carry a bundle of washing for a woman on her way home from the Municipal washhouse.

As a young man Chavasse often used to say, "Because of a stammering tongue, a humpy back, and want of money",[4] he never expected to marry, but he found romance when he was introduced to Edith Maude, a clergyman's daughter. Apparently, they met only twice before he proposed marriage to her in a letter, and they were married on his thirty-fifth birthday in September 1881.

On the occasion of their silver wedding anniversary in 1906, the Diocese presented the couple with a gift of silver plate and a fine old English clock with cathedral chimes. In response to these generous gifts, Chavasse told his audience how they began married life in a tiny house in Oxford and now, in contrast, they lived in a palatial house in Abercromby Square; "and my only complaint is that the house is so large that when I want her it takes me a considerable time to discover in what room she is".[5] Throughout their married life, Edith was a devoted companion and helpmate to her husband, attending Diocesan engagements with him, taking a personal interest in Diocesan organisations, particularly the Mothers' Union and the Sunday School Institute, and often being concerned that the Bishop worked too hard.

The Bishop enjoyed his work, but when he took time off, he loved to read poetry and the English classics and to study maps and guide books. For their summer holidays the family enjoyed going to Northumberland and North Wales, where they could quietly share the beauty of the countryside.

A NEW CATHEDRAL

At his first Diocesan Conference, the Bishop in his address asked everyone to be "patient with me....I shall make mistakes, I shall have much to learn. But till confidence and patience come give me a patient trial". He paid tribute to his predecessor's achievements, especially his church building programme and his success in increasing the number of clergy in the Diocese. Ryle did not build a Cathedral, but he did prepare the way for it, and Chavasse now believed that the time was right to again think about building a new Cathedral, which will be "a visible witness to God in the midst of a great city".[6] In a quiet way he reprimanded the benefactors and citizens of Liverpool, who had built such a magnificent building as St George's Hall, but appeared to be content with St Peter's, a Corporation church, as the Cathedral Church of the new Diocese. His vision of and enthusiasm for a new Cathedral was both an inspiration and a challenge to the people of Liverpool and the whole Diocese. It led almost immediately to a special meeting being called in the Town Hall by Lord Derby to consider the viability of the proposal. In a stirring address the Bishop expressed his vision of "a Church of the people, where rich and poor meet together to worship God, and where the gospel of the Lord Jesus Christ is fully preached....(and whose) walls and towers rising high above the city must be a silent but majestic witness to God and the Unseen". Before the meeting closed a new Cathedral Committee was appointed; a public appeal for funds was launched and the decision made to petition Parliament to grant a new Cathedral Act. The Bill received the Royal Assent in August 1902 and work began on plans to raise a Cathedral worthy of a great city and "the very best that Liverpool and the Diocese could afford".[7]

The Site Committee considered five chosen locations and finally agreed that the best possible site was St James' Mount, where St James' Church once stood. It is a commanding situation, beautiful in elevation, and standing on a high ridge of sandstone overlooking the city and river. Known locally as Quarry Hill, it was the site of an old quarry, and on old maps of the town it is named Mount Zion. Many considered it an ideal location for a Cathedral and symbolic that it was to be built "on the rock".

The next important task was to appoint an architect. Several noted Church architects were invited to submit plans, and among them Sir William Emerson, whose design had won the competition in Ryle's day. He was quietly confident that he would be re-appointed, but he was not successful. It so happened that the Assessors were attracted to "Design No: 1", submitted by a Giles Gilbert Scott, a young London architect, who had no great qualifications, but whose design combined a power and beauty, "which makes a great and noble building".[8] However, the Cathedral Committee, while feeling duty bound to follow the recommendation and appoint a virtually untried architect, asked Sir William Forwood to write to the architect regretting they were unable to accept his design since it did not seat a congregation of three thousand. The *Church Times* suggested this was not the real reason for rejecting Scott. Yet again, the Committee had second thoughts over the appointment of the architect.

GILES GILBERT SCOTT

The appointment of a an inexperienced architect, little more than twenty-one years of age, to be responsible for such an important project, aroused a great deal of adverse criticism. And that was not all. When it became known that Gilbert Scott did not belong to the Church of England, there were loud protests that a Roman Catholic had been selected to design the new Anglican Cathedral.

The appointment might have turned out a disaster, but in reality it was most fortuitous. Scott designed a Cathedral which has been acclaimed as one of the great masterpieces of the twentieth century. To pacify some of those who had doubts about Scott's ability, the Committee judiciously appointed G. F. Bodley, a distinguished architect of wide experience, to oversee Scott's plans.

A local firm of building contractors, William Morrison and Sons, were awarded the first contract to lay the foundations of the East end. Their workmanship was of the highest standards and so impressed that an open contract was given to the firm to carry out the work until the Cathedral was completed. The huge blocks of sandstone were transported by teams of horses and carts from a quarry in Woolton, belonging to Lord Salisbury, and were cut to size by masons on the Cathedral site. Some of the apprentice stone-masons taken on in the early days became fine craftsmen and worked all their lives building the Cathedral.

Work on the foundations proceeded apace and the foundation-stone was laid by King Edward VII, accompanied by Queen Alexandra, at a great ceremony on 19 July 1904. Seven thousand spectators witnessed the festive occasion seated on a huge wooden amphitheatre. The foundation stone, weighing five and a half tons, the gift of the Mothers' Union in the Diocese, was symbolicly laid by His Majesty with a golden trowel and an ivory mallet. The Archbishop of York, the Bishop of Liverpool and several other bishops took part in the celebratory service, which concluded with a choir of a thousand voices singing The Hallelujah Chorus from Handel's Messiah.

CONSOLIDATION

Scott's partnership with Bodley was not always harmonious and when Bodley died in 1907, Scott became the sole architect and now felt free to alter his designs. From this time on, he was continually revising and improving the plans as his skill and expertise matured until his finished masterpiece was different in many respects from the original. The most fundamental change he made was to abandon the idea of twin towers in favour of a great central tower, which allowed for a large central space between the Tower and the two Trancepts, which future Deans have used imaginatively in worship.

In the original plan, the Lady Chapel was to be sited at the west end of the Choir, but Scott decided to place it on the south side and balance it with the Chapter House on the north side. The Lady Chapel, larger than many parish churches, reveals the influence of Bodley in its neo-Gothic design and furnishings, and was consecrated on St Petes Day, 1910, by Bishop Chavasse, in the presence of two Archbishops., twenty bishops, diocesan clergy and civic dignitaries. Because space in the Chapel was limited on the appointed day, the Bishop arranged for twelve special services to be held in the Chapel during the next two weeks, at which sermons were preached by eight bishops, who had had connections with the Diocese in the past. No less than eight thousand worshippers took the opportunity of attending the celebrations.

Work on the Cathedral continued and there were confident hopes that it would be completed within seven years, but the outbreak of the Great War brought the laborious construction almost to a standstill. An interesting letter of the period reveals that the Cathedral Committee agreed in June 1913 to raise the wages of bricklayers, joiners and masons from 10½ d to 11d per hour in November, and navvies and general labourers on site to receive 6d per hour, backdated to September 1912.

CHURCH HOUSE

Church House, situated on a magnificent site, on the corner of Lord Street and South John Street, in the centre of Liverpool, was opened by Lord Derby at the beginning of the century. The building housed several Diocesan agencies, including the Board of Finance, the Board of Biblical Studies, the Church of England Temperance Society, and the Diocesan Sunday School Institute. The Bishop had a room for interviews in the office of the Legal Secretary and Church House soon became a popular meeting place for the clergy and a training centre for the laity.

Part of the top floor was lined with bookcases to accommodate the Bishop Ryle Library, which the late Bishop had generously bequeathed to the Diocese. The Library was established by the efforts of Archdeacon Spooner and Canon H. Mitchell the vicar of Prescot with the wholehearted support of the late Bishop. The volumes were chiefly theological and were designated for the use of the clergy and laity in the Diocese. The collection of books filled most of the shelves and the remaining space housed volumes belonging to the Liverpool Clerical Society and individual donations. In all, the Library had a valuable collection of some ten thousand volumes. In 1903 George Harford, the honorary Librarian, took on a mammoth task, and published a catalogue of all the books in the Library. Unfortunately, some years later the Library was broken up and dispersed and those that remained were destroyed in the Blitz.

CONSOLIDATION

SECTARIAN STRIFE

Chavasse arrived in Liverpool just at a time when the city was plunged into a decade of bitter clashes between the religious fanatics. The streets became a battleground as Protestant and Catholic agitators looking for trouble roused bitter passions. It was estimated that 58% of the Catholic population of England and Wales lived in the area

One well-known advocate of the Protestant cause in the city was George Wise, founder of the British Protestant Union, who led an aggressive campaign against Romanism, Ritualism and Infidelity. He was disappointed that Ryle had failed to stamp out ritualism in the Diocese and he was not confident that Chavasse would be any more successful. He urged his supporters not to contribute a penny towards the cost of building the new Cathedral until the Bishop gave an assurance that it would not be used for ritualistic services.

His speeches at public meetings were often inflammatory, leading to skirmishes with rival groups, and several times he was arrested by the police and charged with a breach of the peace. Wise and other leading Protestant speakers were able to attract thousands of supporters to their rallies and inevitably these street meetings aroused strong opposition from Catholic objectors, and only the timely intervention of the police prevented serious injuries and street riots.

About this time, John Kensit, the celebrated Protestant advocate, and his son, planned to hold a campaign on Merseyside. At a large meeting, convened on Islington Square, in a densely populated Catholic area of the city and close to St Francis Xavier Catholic Church, the younger John Kensit claimed that there were thirty-four ritualist priests in the Diocese and they were working for union with Rome. Protestant supporters clapped and cheered his speech, but a Catholic section of the crowd jeered and threatened to attack their opponents and only a large police presence kept them apart. Similar scenes took place on another occasion on St George's Plateau and arrests followed. Kensit appeared before the magistrates because of his turbulent speeches and given a choice of a fine or imprisonment. Imprisonment made heroes, and Kensit was happy to go to prison for a few days.

Meanwhile his father was holding meetings in Birkenhead and one evening after addressing a huge rally he was walking down to the Ferry to return to Liverpool, when he was struck on the head with an iron bar and suffered serious injuries. He was taken to the Royal Infirmary, but died a couple of weeks later. A young lad, a Roman Catholic, was arrested by the police and charged with attempted murder, but he was acquitted on the grounds that it could not be proved that the blow he struck was really the cause of death.

Another popular venue for Protestant rallies was St Domingo Pit, in the heart of Protestant Everton. Sometimes Catholics demonstrated their solidarity by attempting to hold their rallies at the same meeting place. On one occasion, Wise arranged an anti-Catholic meeting for the same time and the police immediately feared a riot if the two opposing sides clashed at the Pit. A serious disturbance was certainly avoided by the prompt action of the police, though there were some skirmishes and several malcontents arrested for brawling. The arrests only spurred on the Catholics to renew their efforts and later the same day some eight thousand Catholics marched on St Domingo Pit and the police were hard-pressed to disperse them.

It was a long established custom in the city for Roman Catholics to celebrate the patronal festival of their parish church by placing a statue of the Virgin Mary and Child, surrounded by lighted candles, in the front windows of their terraced houses. Sometimes it was reported that the Host was to be carried by the priest in a procession through the streets of the parish, which was contrary to law, and then the Protestant supporters would immediately organise "a monster demonstration" in protest. Fighting would break out between opponents, and sometimes against the police, and those arrested would be charged with riotous behaviour.

It was recorded at this time that Protestant carters, who had to go to work through Catholic districts to reach the docks, were often intimidated and sometimes beaten-up. One newspaper report told how three carters were returning home after work when they were set upon. Two of them managed to break free and escape, but the third was viciously beaten and later died from his injuries. On another occasion a carter was attacked and had to leave his horse and cart and run to hide in a loft until the police arrived.

In some Protestant districts Catholic women and children were often harassed by groups of youths and young children. From an early age children of both denominations learned to ridicule and scoff at each other. When a fight broke out between rival children at St Polycarp's Church School and the neighbouring St Anthony's Catholic School, even the opposing mothers joined in until the police arrived and separated them.

Chavasse naturally supported the Protestant cause, but when he read of some of the violent incidents perpetrated by Protestant zealots in the city, he spoke out against them and wrote to the press expressing his deep sense of shame. This godly and gracious man could be very strict and direct at times, and in a letter to *The Times*, he wrote denouncing the riots and disturbances in Liverpool, which make 'the great name of "Protestant" stink'.[9] He wished to see a more tolerant attitude and in 1911, at Lord Derby's invitation, he joined a small committee of conciliation, including Archbishop Whiteside and George Wise, in an attempt to end sectarian feuding and create a greater sense of harmony among the denominations.

Relationships between Protestants and Roman Catholics at this period were cool, but some clergy were on friendly terms with the parish priests, notably Canon Major Lester, the evangelical vicar of St Mary's Church, Everton, and Monsignor James Nugent, the revered priest of the Catholic Institute, who had a good relationship and occasionally found it possible to work together on some educational or social project.

SUNDAY SCHOOLS

The Diocese took a great interest in the work of education and treated Church Schools and Sunday Schools as major constituents of the Church's work. Chavasse valued this aspect of the Church's ministry and often spoke in enthusiastic terms of the dedication of teachers and the importance of their Christian witness among children and young people. He preferred Church to Board Schools and at the General Election in 1910, he spoke out on the issue, and urged voters to support candidates, who were in favour of Church Schools and Christian education and opposed to dis-establishment

Sunday Schools in the Diocese were one of the Church's healthiest agencies. The Diocesan Sunday School Institute did commendable work in training teachers and providing them with suitable material for their classes. Graded lesson notes were published, together with Bible pictures illustrating the lessons. The annual Teachers' Examination encouraged the laity to take their teaching seriously and helped to raise the standards of religious and moral teaching in the schools. Class teachers were expected to visit their scholars periodically in their homes, especially if they were sick or had missed attending for more than one Sunday.

Children took a pride in learning the set text for the week, repeating it before the teacher and then receiving an illustrated text card as a reward.

During the week many churches provided activities for the young people such as the Band of Hope, the Girl's Friendly Society, the Boys Brigade, and the Church Lad's Brigade. The laity provided enthusiastic leaders and helpers in all this work, and the clergy found that these organisations helped to provide them with a regular supply of young candidates for Confirmation.

During the year there were a number of special events which aroused great interest among the children. The Sunday School Anniversary was one of the highlights of the Church's year. The Childrens' Choir, specially formed for this occasion, rehearsed the hymns and anthems in preparation for the great day. Admiring parents and friends filled the church for the special services and usually a visiting clergyman preached the sermons and perhaps gave "a lecture" to adults the following evening.

No Sunday School Anniversary was complete without "the Walk" through the streets of the parish by all the members of the Sunday School. Generally a band led the procession, followed by the clergy and the Sunday School banner, beautifully embroidered with a text, such as "God is Love" or "Suffer little children to come unto Me", carried by two strong parishioners. Parents and neighbours lined the streets, smiling and waving to the children as they passed by. The annual Procession was not only a Christian witness to the work of the Church among children, but it was also a useful means of publicity and recruitment to the Sunday School.

Most churches organised special activities for the children at Christmas. Nativity plays put on by the children were very popular and, of course, the annual Christmas Party with tea, jelly and cakes, and a visit by Father Christmas (often recognised by the older children as one of the Sunday School teachers), with a bag full of toys and presents to distribute, were unforgettable experiences. In the summer the most exciting event for the youngsters was the Sunday School Treat. For many poor children, who lived in the courtyards and back streets of the city, a trip to the country or the seaside was a new experience. Sometimes the children might be taken by train to Southport for the day, or across the Mersey on the Ferry to the sands at New Brighton, or be carried on a horse-drawn waggonette into the country. The picnic of sandwiches and cakes were prepared beforehand by the teachers and helpers and the outing was always a happy and exciting time.

The amount of activity in the parish on Sundays and weekdays was often considered a barometer of its spiritual life. But the Church at this time had to face the challenge of secularism. More and more people were going out for the day on Sundays and taking their children with them. There were regular band concerts in the parks, museums and art galleries were popular venues, and cheap excursion by rail to the seaside attracted thousands. The Church was unable to hold back the rising tide of secularism and materialism on the Lord's Day and year by year attendances at Church services and Sunday Schools gradually declined.

Addressing an audience of Sunday School teachers in the Diocese, on one occasion, Chavasse said that before he married Mrs Chavasse, she had been a Sunday School teacher for many years, and he added, Today when I am sitting in a railway carriage or walking along a busy street, I am frequently hailed by some one who, thrusting a big, boney hand into mine, will say, "I was in your missus's Sunday School fifty years ago".[10] The Bishop, who had devoted so much of his life to the teaching ministry, recognised a valuable asset in the Church's use of the laity in teaching and training the young in Christian principles, which often bore fruit in adult life.

THE BISHOP'S INNOVATIONS

Chavasse sparked-off several changes in the Diocese which proved worthwhile. Among them was the publication of the Diocesan Gazette, the official publication of the Lord Bishop, which sold in huge numbers at one penny per copy. The monthly journal included the Bishop's Letter, news about the Cathedral, Parish notes, Clerical changes in the Diocese, and lists of Confirmations and Ordinations. The magazine had a wide circulation and continued for many years.

The Bishop established at Church House in 1906 the Board of Biblical Studies. Working in close conjunction with University College, qualified lecturers gave instruction in Biblical Languages, the Old and New Testaments, and Ecclesiastical History, to any clergy or lay person who wished to enrol. Chavasse believed the Bishop should be the chief Shepherd in the Diocese, whose task it was to feed the hungry sheep, and when the Cathedral was completed he hoped to see rooms set aside where groups could study the Word of God together.

When new housing estates began to be developed outside the city boundaries, Chavasse appointed the Bishop's Commission to examine how the Church could meet the needs of the growing suburbs. The Commission recommended the closure of six city-centre churches, where congregations had dwindled and the building of several new churches and halls in districts where there was a greater need. Among those erected, as a consequence of the Report, were Holy Trinity, Southport, St Mary's, Widnes, and St Paul's, Stanley.

The Cathedral Act stipulated that when part of the new Cathedral was made available for services, then St Peter's pro-Cathedral should be closed. Eventually the church was pulled down and the Ecclesiastical Commissioners sold the site to the City Council for commercial purposes, but many Liverpudlians, who worked in the nearby offices, missed the quiet gardens surrounding the Cathedral in Church Street.

The Bishop's Fund, which he set up early in his Episcopate to raise the sum of

£100,000 within five years for Diocesan needs, fulfilled its object. In addition to raising clergy stipends, it helped to provided the means of engaging more clergy and full-time lay workers in the parishes.

THE NATIONAL MISSION

The Great War revealed some of the Church's strengths and weaknesses. Some churches showed signs of spiritual revival and growth as more people attended to pray and seek comfort during the dark days of war, but there was a wide-spread apathy and indifference to religion and it was obvious that the influence of the Church on the Nation was declining. Some believed that God had allowed the War as a judgment on the nation's sins, while others turned away from God, blaming him for permitting the bloom of youth to suffer and die on the battlefield.

In an effort to meet the underlying spiritual needs of the nation and halt the drift away from the Church, the two Archbishops, in the autumn of 1916, inaugurated The National Mission of Repentance and Hope. The aim of the Mission was to move "the men and women of England to earnest and honest repentance of our sins and shortcomings as a nation and to claim that in the living Christ, in the loyal acceptance of him as the Lord of all life, individual and social, lies the one sure hope". The countrywide Mission was intended to involve the whole Church, clergy and laity in partnership and without any party bias. The Archbishops were concerned that the Mission of Witness should be an on-going event and not just limited to an event in November so that the leaven of Christianity might begin to permeate every level of national life.

Chavasse took up the Archbishops' challenge and urged all the parishes in the Diocese to play their part. He made a point of visiting every rural-deanery and speaking on the theme of "Consecration", and stressing that the gospel message of the Cross is the only hope for the individual and the nation. No less than one hundred clergy volunteered to be the Bishop's Messengers and preach in any parish where they were invited. Parishes were free to call on the "Diocesan Messengers" or invite a missioner from outside the Diocese.

The majority of parishes supported the Mission with varying degrees of enthusiasm. Large meetings were held in the town centres and special services in the participating churches. Missioners addressed businessmen in the Stock Exchange, the Corn Exchange and on Exchange Flags, spoke to stevedores and carters at the docks and street corners and to women at their weekly meetings in church halls.

When the ten day Mission ended and the results were assessed in the Diocese, the parishes reported that regular church members had undoubtedly been encouraged and many had shared their faith with others; lapsed members had returned and some clergy had been cheered, but, overall, it was felt that there had not been a revival of faith, which was disappointing after all the preparation and prayer that had been put into the Mission. The final Report on Evangelism concluded that the Mission had been a time of sowing rather than a time of harvest. With this in view the Archbishops set up five evangelistic councils to examine different aspect of the Church's work and foster other ways of spreading the Christian message.

CONSOLIDATION

THE GREAT WAR

In the months before August 1914 the country prepared for War, but did not believe that it would happen. When eventually it was declared that Britain was at war with Germany, the lives of thousands were suddenly and dramatically changed. Men were called up to serve in the armed forces, many of them leaving behind young wives and small children. In Liverpool they rallied to enlist in the King's Liverpool Regiment, and hundreds of volunteers, known locally as The Liverpool Pals, drilled in shirt-sleeves in church halls until their uniforms and rifles arrived. Many of those in reserved occupations worked at the docks, loading and unloading materials for the war effort. Liverpool was an important and busy port on the west coast, and it was known that "Jerry" would try his utmost to disrupt this trade, and more than once it was reported that German submarines had been operating in Liverpool Bay.

War-time was a busy period for the clergy in the parishes and with several volunteering to become army chaplains, it placed an extra responsibility on the rest, who spent much of their time visiting the wounded in hospital and comforting the bereaved. The Bishop wrote hundreds of letters and sent cards to comfort bereaved families in the Diocese, and whenever he learned that one of his clergy had lost a member of the family he went personally to express his condolences and pray with the sorrowing.

Chavasse was a man of peace, but not a pacifist, believing that war is sometimes the lesser of two evils. As a young boy he had ambitions of becoming a soldier, but his illness ruled out that career. Now as his special contribution to the War effort, he was appointed a chaplain to the 5th Battalion of the King's Liverpool Regiment, and went with them to camp in North Wales and even joined them occasionally on their route marches.

The Bishop and Mrs Chavasse had seven children, including two sets of twins, and every one served their country at this time. Dorethea was married to the vicar of St Aldate's, Oxford, and spent much of her time visiting the wounded in hospital; Christopher enlisted as an army chaplain and served in France. Before the end of the War he was awarded the Military Cross and the Croix-de-Guerre for his gallantry in the Royal Medical Corps; his twin-brother, Noel, studied medicine at Liverpool and joined the Liverpool Scottish Regiment. Marjery acted as chauffeur to her father and took him to all his engagements in the Diocese; while her twin-sister, Mary, served as a nurse in France with the Liverpool Merchants' Mobile Hospital, and Aidan, the youngest member of the family, became a lieutenant in the 11th Battalion of the King's Liverpool Regiment.

Every day the *Liverpool Daily Post* contained long lists of Liverpool men who had been killed or wounded in battle. In the summer of 1917 tragedy also struck the Chavasse household. A telegram arrived informing the Bishop that his youngest son, Aidan, was reported "missing and wounded" in Flanders. His death was confirmed sometime later, but his grave was not marked. The news was a hard blow and Mrs Chavasse never fully recovered from the loss. Sadly, within a few weeks they received further news from the War Office that Noel had been killed on the battle-field of France. He had already been awarded the Military Cross and the Victoria Cross for bravery under fire, and it was with great pride and comfort to his parents, they were informed later by Lord Derby that his Majesty had added the bar to Noel's Victoria Cross. They were proud, too, to receive a personal letter written by King George V from Windsor Castle conveying His Majesty's condolences. The confer-ring of the VC and bar was unprecedented during the period of the Great War.

Only a short time before Noel was killed, the Bishop wrote to congratulate him on receiving such a magnificent honour as the Victoria Cross. "You have been known as the son of the Bishop of Liverpool", he wrote, "I shall be known hence-forth as the father of Captain Chavasse".[11] It was with quiet grace and a sorrowing heart that the Bishop personally received the bronze medal with bar on behalf of his son.

There was tremendous rejoicing outside the Town Hall in Liverpool on 11th November 1918, to celebrate the Armistice after four years of bitter slaughter. Thousands stood in the streets cheering and waving flags. but there was a hush dur-ing a short service led by the Bishop, when he offered a prayer of thanksgiving for the end of hostilities.

A Suffragan Bishop

Bishop Royston, whom Chavasse described as "a gracious and saintly personali-ty", retired from the Diocese in 1905, but Chavasse did not consider appointing a Suffragan Bishop to assist him with his episcopal duties until November 1918, when he appointed Canon M. Linton Smith, Rector of Winwick, the first Bishop of Warrington. The office of Suffagan Bishop had been in use in the Church for many years before it was rescinded at the end of the sixteenth century. In 1870 the Act was renewed and several Diocesan Bishops took the opportunity of appointing Suffragans to assist them with the workload in heavily populated Dioceses. Chavasse was now seventy-two years of age, in failing health and aware that in the post-war era the Diocese demanded a greater pastoral oversight. The consecration of the first Suffragan Bishop in the Diocese took place in the Lady Chapel of the Cathedral by the Archbishop of York, Cosmo Gordan Lang, assisted by the Bishop of Liverpool and four other bishops. Bishop Linton Smith was given responsibility for overseeing the northern area of the Diocese on behalf of the Diocesan He was translated to the See of Hereford in 1920 and was succeeded by Canon E. H. Kempson, who came to the Diocese from Newcastle.

The Northern Border

Southport became one of the most popular resorts on the Lancashire coast and as the town grew and prospered, so the churches and chapels proliferated. At the turn of the century, there were sixteen Anglican churches in the Borough, and in 1913 the Mayor claimed that "the number of churches and chapels (in the town) are more than the licensed houses".[12]

St Cuthbert's, Churchtown, is "the Mother Church" of Southport and has been rebuilt several times. In 1908, when the Rev. R. B. Blakeney was Rector, the building was completely gutted in the work of restoration, leaving only the four walls standing. The old chancel was then incorporated into the nave and a new chancel built at a cost of £5,000. In 1917, in recognition of his sterling work, Blakeney was appointed a Canon and made Rural-Dean of North Meols. A new reredos was installed a few years later, along with some fine oak panelling in the chancel, and in 1923 the church celebrated its 700th birthday. Canon Blakeney, a robust character, was Rector of the parish for forty-two years and died in 1948.

Christ Church, in the town centre, was consecrated in 1821 by the Bishop of Chester. On the departure of the Bishop after the service, the sporting vicar, William Docker, and members of the congregation, retired to Barlow's on Lord Street for a celebratory banquet. Later the church developed an evangelical tradition in Ryle's day and has been served by a succession of strong evangelical clergy; among them J. H. Honeyburn (1900-1912), a fine scholar, who was responsible for building the school behind the church; the Ven. J. J. Madden (1912-1916), Archdeacon of Liverpool; J. T. Inskip (1916-1919), who became Bishop of Barking and E. W. Mowll (1919-1928), who resigned on his appointment as vicar of St Aldate's, Oxford.

Holy Trinity, built in 1837, was replaced early in the 1900s with a new church, to become "one of the glories of Southport". The new church, built of red brick with Portland and Bath stone dressings, and with a beautiful nave, the gift of Mr and Mrs Elder of the Elder Shipping Line, is a magnificent edifice. The completed church was consecrated by Bishop Chavasse on 12 March 1912. Installed with a fine organ, Holy Trinity soon developed a great musical tradition in the town. The superlative tower, a Southport landmark, was finished the following year. The first vicar was C. S. Hope, who served in the parish for thirty-three years and retired in 1909. He was succeeded by F. L. Coulson Parkyn (1909-1918), C. B. Hulton (1918-1922) and A. B. Thornhill (1922-1929).

St Luke's, originally a chapel-of-ease attached to Holy Trinity, became the Anglo-Catholic church in the town. It was built in 1880, but not consecrated for another two years. The richly ornate chancel with its seven-sided apse, each with a lancet-window, focuses the worshippers attention on the priestly ritual. In 1904 a regular early morning Communion service was introduced and in 1915 Sung Eucharist replaced Matins on Sunday mornings. In 1926, an aumbry was installed for the Reservation of the Sacrament. The first Vicar, W. H. Marsden (1882-1903), was a former curate of Christ Church; he was followed by G. Richardson (1903-1914), then the Hon. S. G. W. Maitland (19814-1919), an extreme ritualist, and finally in this period, G. H. Thompson (1919-1945).

St James, Birkdale, stood alone in the sand dunes when it was consecrated by the Bishop of Chester in 1857, but it was soon surrounded by many fine residences. The church has the appearance of a village church and is unusual in that it has no pillars in the nave blocking the view of the pulpit and chancel. In 1917, Canon J. B. Lancelot was appointed vicar in succession to Canon J. Hodgins. Lancelot was ordained in 1888 and came to the Diocese as Principal of Liverpool College. He was made a Canon in 1913 and the Bishop's Examining Chaplain in 1921. Serving in the Diocese throughout the whole of the Chavasse period, he worked closely with the Bishop and wrote the official biography, of F. J. Chavasse, and in collaboration with J. W. Tyrer, Chaplain to the Bishop, wrote *A History of the Diocese* for the Jubilee number of *The Liverpool Review*.

Emmanuel Church, completed in 1898, was the last church in the Diocese to be consecrated by Bishop Ryle. Built in the English Gothic style and with a minster-like tower, it was said to be "one of the finest modern churches in the country".[13] The first vicar was Canon J. Denton Thompson, who moved down the road from St Cuthbert's, Churchtown. It had been his desire to close the old St Cuthbert's so that Emmanuel might become the new parish church of North Meols, but local objections were too strong. In 1906 he was appointed Rector of Birmingham, and in 1912 consecrated Bishop of Sodor and Man. Another notable vicar, appointed a little later, was F. W. Dwelly (1916-1925), a gifted liturgiologist, who in 1925, became the first Dean of Liverpool Cathedral.

RETIREMENT

At the end of the War, Chavasse, now seventy-two years of age, seriously considered resigning from the See, believing that it was an appropriate moment for his successor to take charge and steer the course of the Diocese in the decisive years ahead. But when it became known that the Bishop was contemplating retiring from the See, several influential voices persuaded him that his wisdom, foresight and leadership were still needed. There was an immense feeling of love and affection for the Bishop and his wife, and many stories were told of their kindnesses, especially to clergy families. At Christmas time they gave gifts to the poorer clergy and arranged parties for the children at the Palace. At all times the Bishop was ready to visit any sick clergy in the Diocese and prepared to conduct their Sunday services.

It was a great joy to the Bishop and Mrs Chavasse, when he reached the Jubilee anniversary of his ordination and the Diocese marked the occasion with a great celebration in St George's Hall, with the Archbishop of York among the invited guests. During his Episcopate he enjoyed good relations with the Free Churches and he was delighted that their representatives were present in his honour. To his great surprise and to the accompaniment of loud cheers he was presented at the close of the evening by a grateful people with the gift of a new motor car.

There was a feeling of disappointment, however, when eventually Chavasse decided that chiefly because of age and infirmity he must retire from the See. He was now seventy seven years of age, naturally less active than he used to be and becoming more and more dependent on his Suffragan to fulfil episcopal duties Moreover, the next stage of the Cathedral was nearing completion and he believed the new Bishop should preside over the consecration of the Cathedral Quire and Eastern Trancepts. There was also a more personal reason; Mrs Chavasse was not well, becoming physically weaker and requiring constant care. They intended to return to Oxford for their remaining years, where they could enjoy some rest from the demands of the episcopal office and enjoy the benefits of seeing their son, Christopher and his family, in the nearby parish of St Aldate's.

CONSOLIDATION

When the time came for them to leave, presentations were made to both the Bishop and Mrs Chavasse in the Town Hall, in appreciation of all the loving service they had given to the Diocese. The Bishop received an illuminated address and a cheque for £3.807 and Mrs Chavasse, a silver tea and coffee set. In return, the Bishop warmly thanked the clergy and laity in the Diocese for their loyalty and support over twenty-three years, and "Now", he confessed, "my heart almost breaks at the thought that I am going to leave you, but I rejoice... that God has sent you a bishop who will more than fill my place... and I ask you from the bottom of my heart to do all you can to help Dr David to carry on the work in this dear and great Diocese".[14]

Throughout his long Episcopate, Chavasse remained true to his evangelical beliefs; he was a sound churchman, a thoughtful preacher and a born pastor. And in recognition of his outstanding ministry and leadership in the Diocese over two decades, the University conferred on him an honorary degree of Doctor of Law.

On returning to Oxford, Dr and Mrs Chavasse took up residence in St Peter's House, the old Georgian Rectory, which had been their earlier home, and the Bishop looked forward to doing some teaching and pastoral work among the undergraduates. It was a special joy to start again a Greek New Testament class on Sunday evenings and to receive invitations to preach in the local churches. And it was an added bonus for both of them to see their grandchildren almost everyday. Writing to a friend about this time, he said, "My life at Liverpool seems a pleasant dream, from which I have awakened to find myself in Oxford".[15]

The Bishop and Mrs Chavasse received invitations to attend the consecration of the Cathedral Quire in the presence of King George V and Queen Mary and it was a great disappointment when illness prevented them attending. In a letter to an old friend, Chavasse admitted, "My heart was in Liverpool all that day".[16] On a later occasion, when he was on holiday in North Wales, he did have the pleasure of being driven over to Liverpool to see the progress of the new Cathedral and at the same time have the joy of baptising the youngest of his grandchildren in the Lady Chapel. On the eve of his eightieth birthday he preached for the last time in the Cathedral to a large congregation.

It was while the Bishop was doing duty for a sick clerical friend in a parish outside Oxford that Mrs Chavasse was taken ill and a few days later she died quietly in her sleep. So closed a long and singularly happy life together. "Weep I must", he said, "but I continually bless and praise God for giving me such a wife for forty-six years and granting her such an end".[17] After a simple service in the Cathedral, she was laid to rest in the Founders' Field.

The Bishop missed his wife tremendously and only a few months later on 11 March 1928, he, too, passed into the presence of his risen Lord. His body was taken to Liverpool to lie in state in the Cathedral, and thousands passed by as a mark of love and respect for "the peoples' Bishop". Two days later "the saintly Bishop" was interred beside his wife, under the shadow of the great Cathedral he had worked so hard to create.

Dr William Temple, the Archbishop of York paid tribute to Chavasse a few days later at a Memorial Service, saying: "There are few men and not all great men among them, who can see their life's work pass into a successor's hands, and be content. He was great enough to stand aside and be content. He was great enough to stand aside and watch his own work grow". Working people in Liverpool called him "a saint and holy man", and a tramguard publicly testified: "Look at him, look at him - a saint - one of the last of them; you may never see another". The gentry, too, paid tribute to a beloved Bishop. Sir William Forwood, who knew the Bishop as well as anyone, wrote of him, "He came nearer to my ideal of a *Saint* than any man I ever met or heard of, and I saw him under the most trying conditions, yet he never wavered, but always looked upwards, and even heaven itself is today richer for his presence".[18]

It was felt in the Diocese that some lasting Memorial to the late Bishop should be created and placed in an honoured niche in "his Cathedral". It was agreed that a bas-relief representation of the Bishop kneeling in prayer would be appropriate; that a parish church should be built on one of the new estates and dedicated the Bishop Chavasse Memorial Church (Christ Church, Norris Green), and a fund opened to establish St Peter's Hall, Oxford, for undergraduates with modest means, which had long been the Bishop's dream. It was opened in 1929, with Christopher Chavasse, the first Master.

Bishop Chavasse maintained the Protestant and Reformed character of the Diocese and by his quiet and gracious manner consolidated the work begun by his predecessor. During his Episcopate, work began on the new Cathedral; twenty-one new churches were built, many of them in the growing suburbs and greater use was made of the laity, particularly through the new PCCs, which were intended to encourage elected members "to co-operate with the incumbent in the initiation, conduct, and development of Church work both within the parish and outside". His contribution to the life and work of the Diocese was outstanding and enduring.

Chapter 4

ORGANISATION

The population of Liverpool rose to eight hundred and five thousand in 1921. Many families were still living in overcrowded conditions as in Victorian times, but the Corporation was tackling the problem by demolishing derelict properties and providing new homes in the garden suburbs of Fazakerley and Norris Green. A slump in coal mining, engineering and cotton spinning meant that there were no jobs available for the thousands of ex-servicemen, who were looking for work after serving their country, and many were forced to beg on the streets. Conditions worsened and in 1926 the miners, railwaymen, transport and steel workers united in a General Strike at the beginning of May, which lasted for nine days. When others went back to work the miners continued the Strike for better conditions and pay and stayed out until October.

For many years there had been talk in Liverpool about the possibility of building a bridge across the Mersey linking Liverpool and Birkenhead, but nothing materialised. Now the feasibility of a road tunnel under the river was seriously discussed; it would cost a lot of money, but it would provide employment for a huge workforce on Merseyside. The project went ahead and took nine years to complete. It was a great engineering achievement and was opened by King George V in July 1934.

There were fresh challenges to occupy the new Bishop when he arrived in the Diocese. Among the priorities demanding his attention after the War were the completion of work on the Cathedral, a further increase in the number of clergy to meet the demands of the growing population, a necessary rise in clergy stipends and a determination to build the required places of worship and church schools on the new estates.

ALBERT AUGUSTUS DAVID

David's outstanding ability, reforming zeal and organising strengths, marked him out as a young man destined for advancement either in Education or the Church. At Queens' College, Oxford, he gained a double First in Classics and was invited to stay on as a lecturer. He moved on when appointed a tutor at Rugby School and in 1884 was ordained, a requirement of all senior tutors at the School. A year later he became Headmaster of Clifton College, Bristol. He was only thirty-seven years of age when E. A. Knox, the Bishop of Manchester, invited him to become the Suffragan Bishop of Burnley, but he declined. He did, however, accept a post offered him by Bishop Chavasse to be his Examining Chaplain. During these years he received more than one offer of a Bishopric, as well as the Deanery of Manchester, but reluctantly he turned them all down, preferring to remain at Rugby School, where he was now Headmaster in succession to Dr S. R. James.

Shortly before he returned to Rugby, on his appointment as Headmaster, he married Edith Mary Miles, the daughter of a former civil servant in India. She was an ideal headmaster's wife, who gave great support to her husband throughout his teaching career and later ministry. They had three sons and a daughter.

After being in charge at Rugby for eleven years, David was eventually persuaded to relinquish this important post and accept the Bishopric of St Edmundsbury and Ipswich. It was a See recently created and David was only its second Bishop. He was consecrated on the Feast of St James in 1921 by A. F. Winnington-Ingram, the Bishop of London, in Westminster Abbey. Archbishop Davidson, the Archbishop of Canterbury, had followed David's career with great interest over the years. and more than once had offered him preferment and was now bitterly disappointed that illness prevented him from consecrating the new Bishop.

David's precise management of his Diocese from the beginning did not pass unnoticed and within two years, Stanley Baldwin, the Prime Minister, invited him to consider moving from the rural scene of East Anglia to the industrial and grimy clime of south-west Lancashire, with a population four times greater. David had a tenuous link with Liverpool, as the Bishop's Examining Chaplain, and he saw a move to the northern See as a great challenge. When he accepted the Bishopric there was general approval in the Diocese, though some Anglo-Catholics were disappointed that a High Churchman had not been appointed, and some Evangelicals felt that David was a "middle of the road man" and less committed to evangelical principles than either Ryle or Chavasse.

It was an unusual gathering in the Town Hall in October 1923, when the Diocese bade farewell to their beloved Bishop, Francis James Chavasse, and welcomed the tall, dignified Dr David, to Liverpool. It was an occasion of great joy and great sadness. Sadness at the departure of an aged Bishop, who had endeared himself to everyone in the Diocese; rejoicing at the coming of his successor who held the promise of leading the Diocese on to greater achievements and blessings.

A few weeks later Bishop David was enthroned as the third Bishop of Liverpool and Acting-Dean in St Peter's pro-Cathedral and in his first address to an expectant congregation he said it was his desire to offer the right-hand of fellowship to all in the Diocese, whatever their party loyalty, and he gave his friendship to members of the Free Churches as well and wished for a closer bond of unity with them. One of his first appointments was to make the Archdeacon of Liverpool, G. H. Spooner, sub-Dean of St Peter's and responsible for the day to day services

ENTERPRISE

Bishop David came to Liverpool after less than three years in the Diocese of St Edmunsbury and Ipswich and with some clear ideas on making Diocesan administration more efficient. He was a reformer and innovator, who wished to see changes in the patronage system, a reform of the Church Courts and a closer liaison between Religion and Science. As soon as he settled in the Diocese he set about reorganising the various institutions based at Church House and created twelve new Diocesan Boards, responsible for specific aspects of the Church's work. He took a personal interest in the financial affairs of the Diocese and appointed the Rev. C. F. Twichett, then the General Secretary of the Life and Liberty Movement, to be the General Secretary of the Diocesan Board of Finance. Twichett was the Bishop's "chief executive" and they worked closely together in the coming years, The partnership raised huge funds to build several new churches and halls on the new housing estates and renovate a number of Church Schools in the Diocese. Twichett favoured a policy of mortgaging a loan so that the needed buildings could be built and put into use for the benefit of parishioners rather than leaving them without places of worship through lack of funds. Twichett and the Diocesan Board of Finance did not escape criticism for their financial methods, particularly from the voice and pen of Chancellor J. S. Bezzant at the Cathedral, who strongly objected to amateurs being in charge of finances and who made it plain he wished to see experienced lay financiers controlling Diocesan funds. In esteem of his fine work and co-operation, the Bishop made Twichett a Canon in 1928 and when the next vacancy occurred, appointed him Archdeacon of Warrington.

The two Boards of Biblical Studies and Divinity were amalgamated into the Liverpool Joint Board of Divinity. The Joint Board arranged the annual Liverpool Lectures, delivered by an eminent Anglican theologian on some appropriate and relevant subject. In addition, the Board continued to provide courses in religious studies for clergy, lay readers, Sunday School teachers and anyone interested in serious study. These courses took place in various venues: in the Cathedral and Church House principally and in twelve extension centres throughout the Diocese. For those who found it difficult to attend, correspondence courses were available.

A new Board set up by the Bishop and unique to the Church at that time was the Press and Publicity Board, which kept the clergy and laity informed of what was going on locally and in the wider Church. David, a prolific writer, wanted a vehicle through which he could express his views and he launched with the help of the Board, The *Liverpool Diocesan Review* later to become *The Liverpool Review*, a monthly illustrated journal, devoted to religious, social, industrial educational and artistic activities within the Diocese. David usually contributed the first article each month, and this scholarly, informative magazine soon achieved a wide circulation.

It was expected that David, who had devoted himself earlier in life to the work of education should take a special interest in the development of education and training in Christian principles among the young and adults. Before his consecration he had spent thirty years in the teaching profession and had been the Headmaster of two important Public Schools, so naturally, David gave his whole-hearted support to the Diocesan Board of Education and encouraged the Diocese to raise funds for the building of church schools alongside the church on the new housing estates, and to renovate and maintain the older schools in the towns.

He was delighted when the new Warrington Training College and Church Training College for Women was opened in Wavertree in 1930. Founded in Warrington in 1844, the College provided a constant supply of dedicated Christian teachers to meet the needs of the three Dioceses of Manchester, Chester and Liverpool. The new buildings, within easy reach of the city centre, accommodated two hundred students.

ORGANISATION

David was a strong advocate of religious education, both in the home and the school, and was always ready to write an article or address a meeting of teachers on the importance of teaching religion to the young and training them in moral standards. Believing that Religion should have a high profile in the school curriculum, he devoted the whole of the Diocesan Conference in 1929 to the subject of "Religious Education".

THE CATHEDRAL CELEBRATIONS

On 19 July 1924, the twentieth anniversary of the laying of the foundation stone of the Cathedral, the Choir and Eastern Transept were consecrated by Bishop David, in the presence of King George V and Queen Mary. The whole imaginative service was arranged by the Rev. F. W. Dwelly, the vicar of Emmanuel Church, Southport, who had a flair for the ordering of liturgical worship. The Bishop appointed him *Ceremoniarius* to mastermind the whole ceremony, which he did from the opening procession to the final blessing, with a mixture of ancient and modern liturgies and prayers. The entire Service was printed and beautifully bound and followed through without a hitch. However, there was a slight hiccup before the service began. Dwelly was a stickler for punctuality and when the Royal guests arrived early at the Cathedral, Bishop David sent the Dean to ask the King if he would kindly wait a few minutes. Lord Derby attending their Majesty's received the message and protested "The King can't wait", whereupon the Dean replied, "My Lord, the service is not for the King, but for Almighty God". Their Majesties waited while the clergy processed into the Cathedral as arranged.[1] A reporter in the *Manchester Guardian* described the whole event as "an affair of ecclesiastical pomp such as the realm has never seen for many centuries nor for many years is likely to see again".[2]

At a private ceremony after the service, the King graciously conferred a knighthood on Giles Scott, the architect, in recognition of his outstanding work in the creation of the new Cathedral on St James' Mount. It was an honour Sir Giles richly deserved and humbly accepted.

On the following day, the War Memorial Chapel was dedicated by the Bishop in the presence of the King and Queen, and the *Book of Remembrance*, containing four thousand names of men and women in the Diocese who gave their lives in the Great War, was signed by King George.

On the Feast of St James the Apostle, at the end of the full week of celebrations, Bishop David was enthroned in the Cathedral and installed as Acting-Dean.

THE CHURCH CONGRESS

The Congress had previously been held in Liverpool in 1904, and on a unique occasion in October 1926 it convened in the seaside resort of Southport. During the four days of Congress, it seemed to the residents that the town had been taken over by hundreds of clergy. Four thousand delegates attended the meetings in the Winter Gardens and the Pavilion, and at times the traffic was held up in Lord Street, while the long processions of robed clergy made their way from the Town Hall to services in local churches.

The theme of the Southport Congress was *"The Eternal Spirit"*, a subject choice influenced by Dr David, the President of the Congress that year. He was concerned to show that while the Church must be aware of social problems and try to alleviate them, fundamentally, the Church is a spiritual body, entrusted with a spiritual message, and dependent on the Holy Spirit for its life and power. The opening address by the Bishop was broadcast nationwide and, so too, was the Archbishop of York's sermon on Sunday evening from Christ Church. During the days of Congress delegates heard papers on the general theme of The Eternal Spirit, in relation to Nature, Theology and the Church, and the Bible and Evangelism. Some meetings were addressed by women speakers, including Mrs Dwelly, Lady Inskip, and representatives of the Mothers' Union, the Girl Guides, and the Girls' Friendly Society. The Congress concluded with a final service in the Cathedral and a simple Act of Dedication by the whole congregation.

In the twentieth century, the influence of the Church Congress gradually diminished, but the Southport Congress made an indelible impression on all the delegates and on the Diocese, in particular. Deaneries began to work closer together and there was a more sincere and genuine fellowship among the clergy and laity of all schools of churchmanship. The Eternal Spirit was clearly at work.

Herbert Gresford Jones

It was an inspired choice of Bishop David to invite Gresford Jones, the vicar of Pershore, to return to the Diocese as the Suffragan Bishop of Warrington in 1927. He was ordained in the Diocese and served his first curacy in St Helens before being appointed vicar of St Michael-in-the-Hamlet, Toxteth. He held some important appointments during his long ministry, being at one time, Vicar and Archdeacon of Sheffield, Dean-designate of Salisbury, a post which, like Ryle, he never took up, and Suffragan Bishop of Uganda. He was a reliable and trusted friend of David who, particularly in times of crisis, looked to him for support and friendship. Jones had a strong evangelical faith and a keen interest in missionary work overseas. An eloquent preacher, and a Select Preacher at Cambridge on three occasions, he was often sought after to preach at special services and was greatly loved in the Diocese.

PRAYER BOOK REVISION

A Royal Commission appointed in 1904 to consider Ritualism in the Church reported back that "the order of public worship in the Church of England is too narrow for the religious life of the present generation" and in 1923 the Upper House of the Church Assembly introduced, "A Revised Prayer Book (Permissive Use) Measure" and passed it down for consideration to the Lower House of clergy and laity. As a result of these deliberations the Assembly published a Composite Book, to stand alongside the Prayer Book, with some important changes, particularly in the alternative form of Holy Communion, which was then forwarded to Parliament for approval.

Evangelicals were unhappy when they saw some of the alterations and modifications made to the language and order of some services. Protest meetings were called in many parts of the country to halt the steering of the Church in a Catholic and Ritualistic direction. There were fears that the passing of the Measure would legalise the Reservation of the Sacrament, permit the use of wafer bread and the mixed chalice, encourage the wearing of priestly vestments, sanction prayers for the dead, and so radically change the whole ethos and doctrine of the Church of England.

In the Diocese several leading churchmen spoke out in support of the Measure, but the majority voice of Evangelicals, led by the Rev. A. G. Bernard, the scholarly vicar of Emmanuel Church, West Derby, wrote to the press and held protest meetings against the changes. A crowded meeting in the Philharmonic Hall, addressed by Bertram Pollock, the Evangelical Bishop of Norwich, strengthened the hand of Evangelicals, but the controversy only renewed the tension between churchmen.

When the *Deposited Book* was debated in Parliament in June 1928, Mr Hayes, the Member for Edge Hill, Liverpool, stated that tram drivers and ordinary people in his constituency were whole-hearted in their objections and wished to see the Measure voted out. Its eventual defeat was attributed to the efforts of two prominent churchmen, Sir William Joyson Hicks, the Home Secretary, and Sir Thomas Inskip, the Solicitor-General, who both held strong Protestant principles. The Archbishops immediately wrote a Pastoral Letter to all the clergy and laity appealing to them to maintain a propriety and decorum in worship. Bishop David sensing that the controversy might continue to smoulder in the Diocese, pleaded for a spirit of calm and patience, since the Church of England is a comprehensive Church and Evangelicals and Catholics need one another and supplement and complement each other in their ministry.

JUBILEE YEAR

In the Jubilee edition of *Liverpool Review*. the Bishop wrote an article on "The Diocese in 1930", in which he maintained that "the main tradition of the Diocese is Evangelical", although in recent years the number of Anglo-Catholic churches had gradually increased.

In preparation for the Jubilee celebrations, David inaugurated the Bishop's Building Campaign at a meeting in the Town Hall in 1927. On some of the new housing estates there were as yet no Anglican places of worship and the Bishop appealed to the Diocese to raise £250,000 for new buildings. The Great War had delayed an earlier building programme and now there was an urgent need for new churches and parochial halls beyond the inner city boundaries. David sent out "The Bishop's Deputies" to visit every rural-deanery and parish in the Diocese to stir up an interest in the project. The Campaign set off to a good start and within a short time raised £170,000.

In 1930, the Year of Jubilee, the Diocese hoped to raise a further £50,000, through a *One Million Shilling Fund*, one thousand pounds for each year of the life of the Diocese. Large donations were not expected and the Bishop wished to see all church people united in generously making their free-will offering as a Jubilee Thanksgiving. St Luke's, Orrell, was the first church to be built out of the fund, followed by St Andrew's, Clubmoor and St Stephen's, Wigan.

ORGANISATION

In celebration of the first fifty years and all that had been achieved in that time, Bishop David and the Bishop of Warrington, toured the Diocese giving a series of addresses in the Cathedral and parish churches on various aspects of the Church as "the Body of Christ". A survey of the Diocese revealed that, since it's foundation, remarkable progress had been achieved and church people could justly celebrate. In recent years there had been a rise in the number of devout and energetic clergy serving in the Diocese and consequently there was an increase in the number of daily services and administration of the Sacrament on Sundays. In the Cathedral there were special services drawn up annually for the Armed Forces, the Merchant Navy, the University, the Mothers' Union and many other organisations. The Sunday evening non-liturgical services were a tremendous success and attracted large congregations of all ages.

On Sunday 30 July, an impressive service was held in the Cathedral, and attended by a huge congregation, including one hundred and seventy Archbishops and Bishops from all parts of the Anglican Communion. The Bishops were in this country attending the Lambeth Conference and travelled to Liverpool by special train. Alighting at Edge Hill Station, they toured a new housing estate on their way into the city. Before the procession of bishops entered the Cathedral trumpeters sounded the Last Post beside the grave of Bishop Chavasse. Everyone attending the service was presented with *A Welcome Book*, illustrating the work of the Diocese since its foundation. The sermon on the theme of worship in the Early Church was preached by the Archbishop of York, Dr William Temple, who reminded the congregation that the Diocese had the special task of serving an industrial society and dedicating commerce to the glory of God.

During Jubilee Year five new churches were opened, ten parochial church halls erected and seventeen church schools renovated. Yet still there was a demand for more buildings and this led the Bishop to launch his *Seven Year Plan* in 1935, to secure resources to meet the urgent needs of the Diocese in the new districts. He estimated that it would require an additional £35,000 per annum from the parishes. To create an interest in the scheme and gain the needed support, he personally visited every rural-deanery to explain what was required. He asked for "Couriers" to call regularly on parishioners who had promised to give a penny or more a week. Those who had pledged to give were known as *Friends of the Diocese*, and for their gifts they received in return a printed message from the Bishop. David preferred this method of free-will offering rather than depending on Church bazaars and jumble sales to raise Church funds. Unfortunately, the outbreak of War in 1939 abruptly halted any further building and curtailed the collecting scheme. David was disappointed, but rather than leave any estate without spiritual ministrations the Diocese Conference courageously decided to borrow the capital to complete the building programme already begun.

THE UNITARIAN CONTROVERSY

When in 1931 David decided to relinquish the office of Acting-Dean of the Cathedral and set up a Cathedral Chapter, he appealed to the Crown to nominate the first Dean. The Deanery is a Crown appointment and the choice lay between three names: Hugh Richard (Dick) Lawrie Sheppard, Dean of Canterbury, Canon Charles Earle Raven, Canon Residentiary, and Frederick William Dwelly, the Vice-Dean. David favoured Dwelly, who had already shown some of his extensive gifts in arranging several impressive services of worship in the Cathedral, and he was delighted when Dwelly was appointed.

The Bishop had a high regard for the Dean, his artistic gifts and his organising ability, and for his part the Dean sought to provide splendid acts of worship, spiritually uplifting and glorifying to God. He introduced an imaginative use of colour, language and movement into worship in a dignified setting. In partnership with Canon Raven, a member of the new Chapter and Chancellor of the Cathedral, he arranged a series of Peoples' Services at 8-30 on Sunday evenings, which became very popular, attracting large congregations. David sometimes attended these services and wrote of them: "Like many other Cathedrals we attempt to meet the needs of those who by temperament or lack of training cannot find what they want in normal Prayer Book services. Every Sunday evening at half-past eight the building is filled for a non-liturgical service, arranged by the conductor with a view to the subject of his choice, which usually bears upon what people nowadays seem most to want as well as to need, namely, the sense of and expression of worship."[3] Dwelly was gifted in his approach to young people while Raven was a radical and challenging preacher and together they made a great team.

Sadly, in the history of the Church, Bishops and Deans have not always got on well together and David did not always see eye to eye with Dwelly. Perhaps it was that David had been a Headmaster for many years and more recently Acting-Dean of the Cathedral and liked to do things his own way and found it difficult to completely hand over responsibilities to another.

The first major disagreement between the two men was really the Bishop's own making. David was a broad-minded churchman, with a liberal and ecumenical outlook, and he stated that he wished to see the Cathedral open "to all men of good will without regard to creed or manner".[4] The Dean, too, thought that the House of God should welcome Christians of other denominations as well as Anglicans, and with the Bishop's acquiescence he invited Dr Lawrence Pearsall Jacks, the Editor of the *Hibbert Journal*, and a notable preacher, to address a series of three Peoples' Services in the Cathedral in June 1931.

Immediately there were murmurs of discontent in the Diocese that a Unitarian had been invited to occupy the Cathedral pulpit, but Dwelly shrugged off the criticism and the services went ahead. A few months later, the Dean invited the Rev. Lawrence Redfern, a local Unitarian minister, to preach at His Majesty's Judges Assize Service. This was too much for the Rev. Roger Markham, the Rector of Aughton, and other Evangelicals in the Diocese, who wrote strongly worded letters of protest to the *Liverpool Daily Post*, pointing out that Unitarians denied the historic faith of the Church by denying the deity of Christ and therefore should be barred from the Cathedral pulpit. Canon J. B. Lancelot, vicar of St James's, Birkdale, agreed with his colleagues, asserting that "some of us would rather go to the stake than admit them to our pulpits".[5] The Dean's action, was not without some support, however, and Canon Pat McCormick, the famous broadcasting vicar of St Martin's-in-the-Fields, London, wrote to the press stating that since Dr Jacks had preached in his church why not in a Cathedral?

The matter was taken up by Lord Hugh Cecil, an influential laymen in the Church Assembly, who urged David to institute legal proceedings in the Church Courts against the Dean. The Bishop refused to act, but he did instruct Dwelly not to invite any more Unitarian preachers to the Cathedral. Cecil then pressed the Archbishop of York to intervene and at the next meeting of the Joint Synod of Convocation, the President expressed his disapproval of what had happened in Liverpool. However, since Bishop David was absent because of sickness, the matter rested until David had an opportunity to present his own thoughts on the subject

At the next gathering of Convocation, David insisted that Dr Jacks had been invited to the Cathedral as an individual and not as a representative of the Unitarian Church, and that the Services he attended were popular, non-liturgical acts of worship late on Sunday evenings. In the debate which followed, Dr A. C. Headlam, the Bishop of Gloucester, felt that the invitation had been a mistake and "an offence to believing Christians". When the Bishop of Durham, Herbert Hensley Henson, called for a motion of censure barring Unitarians from Anglican pulpits, the Bishops voted unanimously in favour. David graciously accepted the Judgment and it was assumed that that was now the end of the affair.

It came as a shock sometime later when at a service in the Cathedral, a letter was read from the pulpit in the name of the Dean and Charles Raven, Chancellor Emeritus, and now Professor of Divinity at Cambridge, publicly apologising to Dr Jacks " that out of an act of friendship, there should have arisen this outburst of *odium theologicum* is to us a matter of which we are bitterly ashamed". A similar letter of apology was sent to Lawrence Redfern. The Bishop was annoyed and felt that the public apology flew in the face of the York Judgment and suggested to the Dean, that for the sake of peace and unity in the Church he ought to consider resigning. Dwelly felt that he had been misjudged and saw no reason why he should resign, and now the Bishop wondered whether the matter called for his own resignation, but Dwelly urged him not to do so, on the ground that "the difficulties between you and me are not difficulties of purpose or spirit but of method".[6] The Cathedral Chapter also published a statement dissociating itself from the apologies and declaring that no individual member of the Chapter, still less, a former member, had any right to speak in the name of the Cathedral.

The controversy inflicted a deep scar on the Diocese, which was not completely healed until long after the Dean retired in 1955.

THE MERSEYSIDE CRUSADE

For ten days in the autumn of 1933, an Evangelistic Crusade was held in the Diocese, sponsored by the Archbishop of York and the Bishops of Chester and Liverpool. This was an interesting venture and the first time the two parts of the former large Diocese had combined in a United Mission. In Liverpool, David invited the Industrial Christian Mission, which had had many years of experience in evangelism at the docks and in the factories, to spearhead the Crusade. At a press meeting before the Mission began, the Bishop insisted that "it's purpose was not to proselytise on behalf of the Church of England, but to present the message of the gospel in a challenging way, and to combat the increasing materialism of the age". As part of the Campaign it was hoped that the Bishop might be able address the crowd at the forthcoming football match between Everton and Arsenal and also from the boxing ring at the Liverpool Stadium, but the directors cautiously declined permission on the grounds that they were non-sectarian venues.

Some two hundred missioners, from both within and outside the Diocese, were appointed and sent out by the Bishop after the commissioning service in the Cathedral. The majority of churches in the Diocese participated in the Mission under the banner *Christ the Lord of Life*. In addition to all the evangelistic services in churches and parish halls there were numerous open-air meetings at street corners, in factories and theatres and challenging addresses delivered at lunch hour meetings at the dock gates and at the Pier Head.

The Mission met with little sectarian opposition and the Bishop concluded that it had been "a success". The Mission touched some ten thousand people with a fresh and energetic approach to reach those who needed to be challenged with the good news of the Gospel. As a follow-up, the Diocesan Board of Evangelistic Work gave practical support to the parishes by providing them with further attractive evangelistic and teaching material.

A TRIP TO AUSTRALIA

The Bishop had not been well for some time and he and Mrs David took a three month working-holiday to Australia in the summer of 1935. David had been invited to visit Perth, Adelaide and Melbourne as a representative of the Anglican Church for the Centenary Celebrations of the State of Victoria. It was a great joy for him during his visit to renew acquaintants with Frederick Waldegrave Head, the Archbishop of Melbourne, and a former Canon of Liverpool Cathedral. During his stay in Australia he was kept busy preaching, opening exhibitions, meeting the press and broadcasting to the nation, but he enjoyed every moment of it.

Archbishop Downey, the Roman Catholic Archbishop of Liverpool, also sailed on the same ship to take part in the Centenary Celebrations. The long voyage gave the two men an opportunity to get to know each other better, and though they held conflicting views on a number of moral and religious issues, they enjoyed each others' company, both rising early each morning to swim together in the open-air pool.

Meanwhile, the Bishop left the affairs of the Diocese in the capable hands of Dr Gresford Jones, the Bishop of Warrington.

The Bishop and Mrs David enjoyed the leisurely six-week voyage back to the United Kingdom, which included spending Christmas on board, and returned to Liverpool refreshed and rejuvenated to take up their Diocesan responsibilities. They were welcomed back at a reception in the Town Hall arranged by Bishop Jones, at which David announced that he had invited Archbishop Head to visit the Diocese and preach in the Cathedral. The trip had been a learning experience and he was convinced that the Mother Church of England could learn much from the younger Commonwealth churches. In particular, he thought it a good idea to encourage the interchange of clergy from the two countries and to offer some of the unemployed young people in this country the challenge of a new life overseas.

THE BLITZ

The wail of the air-raid sirens sounded for real in the summer of 1940 and for ten months Merseyside and its Docks were the target of the Luftwaffe bombers. The severe onslaught, night after night, was an attempt to destroy the Port and cut off vital supplies of food and munitions from overseas. Liverpool was in the forefront of the Battle of Britain, but the surrounding towns also suffered the bombing and destruction in an attempt to bring Britain to its knees.

The first wave of planes on a raid dropped thousands of incendiaries to light up the way for the following bombers The most devastating attacks were during the eight nights at the beginning of May 1941. On a couple of those nights the bombing lasted from dusk until dawn. Fires raged in the streets of the city and the destruction of the warehouses and sheds lining the Docks could be clearly seen across the bay from North Wales. Among the public buildings damaged or destroyed during the Blitz were St George's Hall, Central Station, the Main Post Office, and the City Museum and Library. The railways and docks were the primary target and at Huskisson Dock the freighter *Malakam*, loaded with munitions for the Middle East, was set alight and blew up before it could be sunk, causing tremendous damage and loss of life.

The Civil Defence Services were stretched to the limits and did a marvellous job fighting the fires, attending to the injured and dying and next day restoring the utility services. In all, there were sixty-eight enemy raids on Merseyside during which nearly four thousand civilians were killed and the same number severely injured. Thousands of homes were destroyed and many were made homeless. Nevertheless, the indomitable spirit of the Liverpudlians never faltered and the next day following a raid, the survivors would set off to work with a rugged determination not to be beaten and to face the new day with characteristic good humour.

Churches and Chapels did not escape the onslaught and the Diocese lost seventeen churches totally destroyed, including St Nicholas Parish Church at the Pier Head, St Luke's Church, Bold Street, Mossley Hill and Walton Parish Churches and hundreds more were badly damaged. Six vicarages were lost and the same number of church halls and schools. The cost of restoring the damaged buildings was estimated to be about £750.000, but the work of re-building could not be undertaken until after the War. It was at this time that Church House was destroyed and important documents relating to the Diocese were lost. Fortunately, temporary accommodation was found in Moorfields to house the Diocesan agencies until suitable premises could be found for a Church House. Eventually a fine corner site in Hanover Street, close to the city centre, was purchased.

It is not surprising that the huge edifice of the Cathedral dominating the Liverpool skyline suffered some damage from enemy action. It is a miracle that it was not completely destroyed considering the many tons of bombs which rained down on the city during the Blitz. Yet, throughout the whole of the War, it stood tall and triumphant, a fitting symbol of the resolute faith and courage of the people.

TURBULENT TIMES

Reference has been made to the clash between the Bishop and the Dean over the Unitarian affair, but this was only one of several altercations which disturbed the peace of the Diocese at this time.

In the summer of 1929, a disagreement between the Bishop and three Anglo-Catholic priests in the Diocese became public knowledge. It transpired that they conducted services in their churches, which David considered contravened the very reasonable conditions he had laid down in permitting the Reservation of the Sacrament, and the priests actually encouraged the adoration of the Host. David was not in favour of extreme ceremonialism and he was not prepared to allow his clergy to introduce a service like Benediction in their churches. He was happy to allow the Reserved Sacrament to be taken to the sick in the parish, but not for the purpose of veneration in church. Some time before, Dr David had revived the Diocesan Synod, a consultative body of Diocesan clergy, which the Bishop occasionally called together as the need arose. This was an occasion when the Bishop wished his clergy to strengthen his hand and the case of the three priests was debated in a special Synod. The Bishop found he was supported by the majority of clergy that the offending priests should be censured for disobedience. The defiant priests refused to recognise the Bishop's ruling and so in his judgment "excluded themselves from the fellowship of the Diocese".[7] He wrote personal letters to the Wardens of the parishes concerned: St Margaret's, Toxteth, St Thomas', Toxteth and St Stephen the Martyr, Edge Hill, stating that since the Bishop had been unable to persuade the incumbents to obey his directions, they were now suspended from Office. Their suspension continued throughout the remainder of David's Episcopate. Some in the Diocese thought that he had acted unjustly since he raised no objections to "Dwelly's Circus" in the Cathedral.

The relationship between the Bishop and Archbishop Downey was cordial but not close, and it was not helped when the Bishop and the Board of Divinity invited Dr G. G. Coulton, a Cambridge theologian, to give the celebrated "Liverpool Lectures" on *Romanism*. The series of addresses obviously pleased some in the audience, but antagonised others who objected to the speakers verbal attack on the Church of Rome. The "Lectures" may have clarified Roman beliefs and practices, but did nothing to enhance the cause of unity in the city. David was a Protestant at heart and saw nothing wrong in a distinguished theologian pointing out some of the doctrinal differences between the Anglican and the Roman Church. He, himself, could not accept the doctrine of the Mass or Papal infallibility, and he protested vehemently against Roman Catholic priests denouncing mixed marriages and insisting that children born of these marriages should be baptised in the Catholic Church.

Since the potato famine in Ireland in the middle of the nineteenth century, the

ORGANISATION

Irish poor tended to migrate in large numbers to this country and settle in Liverpool. David for some time had felt that the city was being overwhelmed by the stream of Irish Catholics landing at the Port, who then being unable to find work, lived off the dole. He believed that their presence stirred up Protestant rankling and embittered communities. Archbishop Downey could not let the Bishop's strictures pass unanswered and a verbal conflict broke out between them. Their letters to each other were seen, when they later appeared in the press, to be turbulent and vitriolic in the extreme, and inevitably the dispute became a national issue.

Toward the close of his Episcopate, David fell foul of one of his own clergymen. Dr W. W. Langford, the Rector of Sefton, who unashamedly made several personal and scurrilous attacks on the Bishop's administration. These were published at monthly intervals in the *Sefton Letters and Papers*, in which the Rector took the Bishop to task for some of his innovations and policies. The charges were hurtful and wounding and did nothing to enhance Christian virtues.

WIGAN DEANERY

Wigan was a settlement even in Roman times and received the Royal Charter only a few years after Liverpool. Mining was an established industry in the area and the town rapidly developed through the Industrial Revolution and, more so, with the opening of the Leeds-Liverpool Canal in 1774, which linked the town with the sea and considerably increased its trade. The Borough has always exhibited a strong Church life, with a particularly strong link between the Church and the School.

All Saint's, the Parish Church, in the town centre, dates back to the thirteenth century, and was rebuilt in 1850, at a time when many churches were being restored and refurbished. Extensive work was carried out on the stonework between 1898 and 1902 and the tower was completely restored in 1922. The Rev. C. C. Thickness was the Rector (1917-1936) and during those years had a great influence and made a deep impression on the religious life of the community. He was a High Churchman, who chose the Patronal Festival in 1922 to restore the use of vestments in services, and introduced a regular Sung Eucharist the following year. Another of his innovations was to place a *Sedilla*, a row of seats for the Celebrant and his assistants, within the Communion rails. His work was recognised, and in 1926 Chavasse made him a Canon of the Cathedral and a few years later he was appointed Dean of St Albans.

The town has a High Church tradition and the Rector is the patron of several churches in the deanery. Among them is St George's (1780), St Andrew's (1882), St Michael and All Angels (1878), All Saint's, Hindley (1641) and St John the Divine, Pemberton (1832). The Rector is also the patron of St Catherine's (1841), which has a pronounced evangelical witness in the town.

All Saint's, Hindley, was in need of extensive renovation after the War and the Parochial Church Council in 1925 drew up plans for a new church. A fund was started a couple of years later, but because of the depression in trade and high unemployment in the area only £365 had been raised after four years. It was decided that instead of a new building, the existing church should be renovated, a new vestry added and the gallery restored. The clergy serving the parish at this time were the

ORGANISATION

Rev. C. J. Buckmaster (1886-1923), the Rev. W. R. Rhys (1923-1936) and the Rev. A. H. Johnson (1936-1952). Johnson produced a parish booklet to mark the Tercentenary of the Church in 1941, in which he records that for one hundred and fifty years the same family in the parish had been sextons and vergers at All Saint's.

St John the Divine, Pemberton, maintained the High Church tradition in the parish. In celebration of one hundred and fifty years of history, the church published an interesting brochure, *Portrait of a Parish*, in which the clergy of this period are named together with a brief resume of their work. The Rev. E. F. Forrest (1887-1922), was vicar for thirty-five years and left his mark on the parish. He published the first Church Magazine in the parish with a circulation of three hundred, and fitted out the choir with white surplices. Surplices were considered "Roman trappings" by some Protestants and it was not long before a disgruntled parishioner got his hands on them and cut them into shreds. The Rev A. Longdon (1922-1930) was the Northern Secretary of the Church of England Mens' Society for ten years and built up the life of the parish after the War. The Rev. A. H. Johnson (1930-1936), a renowned Tractarian arranged huge annual Bazaars to help reduce the debt on the Schools. In 1931 the Bazaar raised a record sum of £830. The Rev. E. Troup (1936-1940), tried to elicit interest in and support for a new church over a seven year period, but without success. However, he did persuade the Diocese to take over the £3.000 debt remaining on the Schools. The Rev. J. H. Bartlett (1940-1950) continued the High Church tradition and started the Family Eucharist on Sunday mornings. He also took an active part in parish affairs and was an enthusiastic supporter of the local football teams and the Pemberton Carnival.

MOVING ON

In March 1944 David announced to the Diocesan Conference that it was his intention to resign from the See in the near future, believing that with the cessation of hostilities in Europe it was the right time to hand over to a successor. Some weeks later representatives of the clergy and laity together with the City Council met together in the Town Hall at the end of April 1944 to make presentations to the Bishop and his wife and to bid them farewell as they left for their retirement home in Cornwall. The Bishop had worked for a Doctorate of Divinity when at Rugby School and now, before leaving the city, the University honoured him in recognition of his fine work by conferring on him an honorary doctorate.

Perhaps David never ceased to be a Headmaster and at the age of seventy he continued to exercise his authority over the Diocese. His authoritarian manner intimidated some clergy and laity, but those who were fortunate to know him warmed to his friendly smile and his genuine interest in all aspects of their parochial ministry. During his Episcopate he raised some £85.000 for the needs of the Diocese. Although Broad and Anglo-Catholic churches were now more widely recognised in the Diocese for their contribution to the religious and social life of the community, the evangelical witness continued to flourish, while a more liberal stance was being adopted by some.

Chapter 5

MISSION

The War changed the face of Liverpool and left the city with an enormous task of reconstruction in the post-War period. It was not likely that the Atlantic traffic so vital to the Port would ever build up again to anything like the heady days of the 1930s, when the Cunard and White Star liners at the Pier Head were filled with out-going and in-coming passengers and the merchant ships in the docks loaded with goods. Within a few years the shipping companies were giving place to the air lines.

The famous Overhead Railway, "The Dockers Umbrella", running for seven and a half miles alongside the many docks, had served its purpose over half a century, and now, since fewer merchant vessels tied-up alongside the huge cranes, the grain stores and transit sheds and the thousands of dockers were no longer required, the service came to an end and eventually the familiar structure was dismantled.

Streets of terraced houses near to the docks had been destroyed during the Blitz and the Council cleared the sites and housed in "pre-fabs" and new houses some of those who had been "bombed out". The Council also discussed the future of the Docks and proposed the development of new industrial estates for light engineering and a diversity of industries which it was hoped would provide new jobs for all the unemployed men and women.

The Diocese came together in 1945 to give thanks to God in a Thanksgiving Service in the Cathedral for the cessation of hostilities in Europe and the Far East and looked forward with cheer and hope to a new era of spiritual growth and expansion under the leadership of the new Bishop.

CLIFFORD ARTHUR MARTIN

Clifford Martin never thought that one day he would be a bishop. He was not ambitious and did not look for or expect any high position in the Church. He was content to be a faithful pastor in the parochial ministry, which he loved so much. Moreover, he was a convinced evangelical, and evangelicals at that time were not often chosen to be bishops. Neither did he have the advantage of a good University degree, since after the War he had to make-do with a short Cambridge degree course for ex-servicemen. He had served in the Royal Sussex Regiment, first as a private and then as a commissioned officer. Unfortunately, due to an accident while cleaning a gun, he lost the sight of an eye and the Army posted him to Cambridge, where he trained cadets in armoury. From Fitzwilliam Hall, where he took his degree, he went on to Ridley Hall to study for ordination. He was ordained in 1920 by Gordan Cosmo Lang, the Archbishop of Canterbury.

For four years he was a curate at Christ Church, Croydon, a well-known evangelical church in South London, and in time, moved on to the Church Missionary Society headquarters in the City as its Youth Secretary. There he met and fell in love with Margaret la Trobe Foster, a secretary in the offices of the Society, and the daughter of a clergyman of Huguenot descent. They were married in 1926 and had one son and three daughters.

When the benefice of Christ Church, Croydon, became vacant, Martin was persuaded to return to the parish as vicar. After some years of conscientious ministry there he moved to the seaside parish of Christ Church, Folkestone, and in 1939 he was appointed vicar of St Andrew's, Plymouth, an important parish in the city centre, and widely known as "Drakes Church".

In addition to ministering to his parishioners, Martin gave himself whole-heartedly to serving the spiritual needs of many of the men and women in the Forces stationed in Plymouth. For three months he witnessed the air-raids on the city and the docks in 1941, during which he saw his own church destroyed and the vicarage severely damaged. Soon after the Blitz, King George and Queen Elizabeth paid an official visit to the city and met Clifford Martin, and shortly afterwards he was appointed Chaplain to the King in recognition of his spiritual leadership and his untiring work among the people.

Quite unexpectedly in 1944, following the retirement of Dr David, Martin was nominated the next Bishop of Liverpool. Most of the people in the Diocese had never heard of Clifford Martin; however, when more became known about him and the outstanding work he had accomplished in Plymouth, he was assured of a great welcome when he arrived in the Diocese

Martin was consecrated Bishop of Liverpool by Cyril Garbett, the Archbishop of York, on St James' Day, 25 July 1944, in the presence of twenty-one bishops and a huge congregation of well-wishers from all parts of the country. The Bishop-elect was presented to the Archbishop by two of his closest friends, Wilson Cash, the Bishop of Worcester, and Charles Curzon, the Bishop of Exeter, and the sermon was preached by Canon M. A. C. Warren, the General Secretary of CMS, and a long-standing friend and colleague of Martin.

Some weeks later the new Bishop was enthroned in the partly-completed Cathedral in Liverpool before a congregation of three thousand at a splendid service specially arranged by the Dean. During the service four hundred clergy gave Martin a personal welcome to the Diocese. In his enthronement sermon, the Bishop spoke of his total dependence on the Lord for the task ahead: "I stand," he said, "in the succession of three great men, Ryle, Chavasse and David. I cannot hope to follow any of these, yet, if God has called me, as I believe he has, then he will use me in the way he chooses". Though he was hardly known in the north of England before he came to Liverpool, it soon became evident to both clergy and laity in the Diocese that he was the right man to lead them.

POST WAR DEVELOPMENTS

One of the first tasks the Bishop undertook was to do something to relieve the isolation and deprivation felt by those living on the new housing estates, who missed the sense of community and neighbourliness they had known in the old streets and courtyards of the city. The estates were not without a Christian witness since the Diocese had appointed several younger clergy to minister in these new areas, but there was a felt need for a church building as a focal point in each community.

MISSION

On several estates the Diocese rented a council house for the use of a clergyman and his family and the front-room was set aside as a meeting place for Worship, Holy Communion, Sunday School, Women's meetings, and Confirmation classes. All took place in these confined, but homely surroundings, but as numbers grew, church members hoped that one day they could build "their own church" for worship.

The Diocese was generous in funding new churches and halls, but the War had placed a heavy burden on resources. At the end of hostilities no less than one hundred and twelve churches had been destroyed or badly damaged, and before they could be renewed or replaced, a claim had to be put before the War Damages Commission. Eventually compensation was paid out and work began on new buildings and the restoration and refurbishment of damaged churches, parish halls and schools. Among the new churches built after the War were St Matthew's, Thatto Heath, and St Mary's and St James', both in Bootle, Walton Church, the ancient Parish Church of Liverpool, was rebuilt and the fine Parish Church of St Matthew and St James', Mossley Hill, restored.

CHARLES ROBERT CLAXTON

On the retirement of Gresford Jones, the Bishop of Warrington, at the close of 1945, Clifford Martin was delighted to appoint him an honorary Assistant Bishop of Liverpool. In his stead he brought Charles Robert Claxton, the Home Secretary of the Missionary Council of the Church Assembly to the Diocese to fill the vacant bishopric. He was consecrated by the Archbishop of York in the Cathedral, and had the distinction of being the first bishop to be consecrated in the new Cathedral. In the Diocese he took a particular interest in youth work and the Sunday Schools Teachers' Association and confirmed hundreds of young people. In addition to his episcopal duties, Claxton was also Rector of West Derby (1946-1948) and Vicar of Halsall (1948-1959). Popular in both parish and Diocese he was known to take a Christmas Eve service in the local public house. He spent a year studying the work of Church and Industry in the Widnes area before leaving the Diocese. His qualities and gifts were recognised and in 1960 he was translated to the neighbouring See of Blackburn.

EVANGELISM

Shortly before he died, William Temple, the Archbishop of Canterbury, with Cyril Garbett, the Archbishop of York. appointed a Commission, under the chairmanship of Christopher Chavasse, the Bishop of Rochester, and a son of the former Bishop of Liverpool, to report back on effective ways in the post-War era of strengthening the faith of the Church and winning for Christ the thousands of men, women and children, who had little or no apparent belief in God. The report was published in 1945 under the title *Towards the Conversion of England* and immediately became a religious best-seller. The aim of evangelism formulated by the Commission has never been put more succinctly: it is "so to present Jesus Christ in the power of the Holy Spirit, that men shall come to put their trust in God through him, to accept him as their Saviour and serve him as their King in the fellowship of His Church".

Martin had a deep concern for the many without Christ and urged clergy and laity alike to make evangelism a priority in their ministry. Our first task as Christians, he would say, is "to deepen our spiritual life in Christ, and in that faith to proclaim the gospel".[1] " He himself was an example and gave a lead to the Diocese in all his ministry. He passionately believed "we have the best news ever made known to man"[2] and he was determined to make it known. Evangelism was a priority in all his ministry.

THE BISHOP'S COMMISSION

Following the publication of *"Towards the Conversion of England"*, Martin commissioned a survey of the Church in the region, which on completion stressed that an urgent necessity was the revival of spiritual life and re-dedication to God. There were signs of activity in the parishes, but little evidence of real growth in the things of God. There was need for the life of the Church to be deepened and invigorated by the Spirit and for Christians to become more effective in their witness. In his Primary Visitation Charge delivered in 1948, the Bishop said he was anxious that the Church, and in particular the Church of England, should come alive with the power of God, and so shine as a light in the world. But he did not feel pessimistic, for the Church is much stronger than her members think she is. It was recognised that the state of the Church was due in part to the shortage of manpower and there was a desperate need to increase the number of ordinands entering the ministry. In 1939 there were one hundred and fifty-three curates and ninety full-time lay workers serving in the Diocese, but a decade later in 1949 the numbers had dropped to forty-three curates and thirty-seven lay workers.

In addition to an increase in manpower, the survey also showed that nineteen new churches should be built where the need was greatest along with twenty-six mission churches and parochial halls. Attention was also drawn to some churches in parishes where most of the population had moved away, leaving them with very small congregations. It was now beginning to be recognised that there was a surfeit of older churches in the inner city area and with a dwindling population and a decline in attendances there was no need for them all. In Everton, for instance, there were no less than eleven churches within an area of two square miles. The upkeep and maintenance of these churches was both costly and inefficient and though it would upset many members who had faithfully supported the churches over the years it was proposed that some should either be closed or united with neighbouring parishes.

As part of the reorganisation, several of the Boards at Church House were amalgamated and the Commission strongly recommended that there should be a greater focus on the Cathedral as the Mother Church of the Diocese, a new emphasis on Diocesan Sunday to publicise the work of the Diocesan agencies and their needs and a wider circulation of *"The Diocesan Leaflet"* among parishioners.

A BOOTLE PARISH

In 1952 the churches in the Bootle Deanery joined with the local Free Churches in the United Bootle Campaign. After several weeks of prayerful preparation the Bishop of Warrington commissioned the missioners and student helpers and sent them out to the various churches as ambassadors for Christ and representatives of

MISSION

the King of Kings. The teams of students visited hundreds of homes with invitations to the Mission and gave their testimonies at the services. A torchlight procession and an open-air rally in a local park were attended by hundreds of church members and attracted a great deal of interest. The Campaign closed with a final rally in Linacre Mission and it became clear that prayers had been answered, many had been converted to Christ and the churches had been given a new vision.

One practical outcome of the Mission was the weekly visit by two local clergy, (one was the Rev. Jim Roxburgh, vicar of St Matthew's, later to become the Bishop of Barking), who went on their bikes to hold open-air meetings for the dockers at the dock gates.

It was appropriate that a parish with more than twenty factories within its boundaries should make something of Industrial Sunday, and each year, exhibits from the local works, such as cables, machinery, leather goods and even tar products, were on display in the church. Civic representatives, managers and workers on the shop floor attended the evening service. On one occasion John W. Laing, CBE, founder of the building and engineering company, preached the sermon, and another year, A. G. B. Owen, Managing Director of the Rubery Organisation, was the guest speaker.

The friendly relations which developed between the Church and Industry led to regular visits to some of the works' canteens, to hold short evangelistic meetings and occasionally show Fact and Faith films. It was not easy to break through the barrier of indifference, but some workers did express an interest in the Christian message and began to talk about their personal problems.

The Coronation of Queen Elizabeth II aroused a great deal of attention and delight, and for the first time those who were not privileged to witness in person the ceremony in Westminster Abbey could view the whole scene on television. Not everyone possessed a television set and parishioners were invited to the Church Hall to see the event on a large (for those days) screen, kindly lent by a local TV shop.

Many of the streets in the parish were decorated for the occasion with flags and bunting and photographs of the Queen Elizabeth and Prince Philip adorned many front windows. The celebrations reached a climax with street parties, dancing and firework displays in the evening.

It added to the joy of the occasion when news was received that the expedition to Everest, the world's highest mountain, had been successful, and Hilary and Tensing had reached the summit.

On the nearest Sunday to St Valentine's Day, the vicar invited those couples who had been married in the church during the past three years to attend a special weekend. Baby sitters were provided for those families who lived in the parish. The Husbands and Wives Service followed closely the Marriage Service and gave opportunity for couples to renew their vows and re-dedicate themselves to God and to each other. On the following evening a Social was held in the Hall during which a wedding cake was cut by the longest married and the most recently married and a photograph taken of the whole assembly

Not all the efforts to reach out to the parish were successful, but the showing of an interesting religious film during Holy Week brought several hundred parishioners and friends to the church. Advertisements in the local press and by posters through-

MISSION

out the parish gave much publicity to the film, and teams of visitors made house to house calls offering free tickets for the evening performances. Three hundred children attended a special early showing of *I Beheld His Glory* on Good Friday evening, and each night of the week the pews were filled with an interested audience. At the close of the evening a simple invitation was given to receive Christ as Saviour and those who responded were helped by trained Christian counsellors.

As part of the outreach to children in the parish, the vicar, with several helpers, held open-air meetings in various streets during the month of August. The sound of an accordion quickly attracted a group of fifty or sixty children, who for the next hour enjoyed singing choruses, taking part in competitions and listening to Bible stories.

The Children's' Mission led by "Uncle Jim" (now Canon Jim Hamilton), gave a great boost to the Sunday School. During the preparations for the Mission the children were repeatedly told to look out for "Uncle Jim", who was coming to the parish. On the Saturday afternoon he was due to arrive, the street outside the Church Hall was thronged with excited youngsters and it took an age to get them marshalled inside and settled down. A gifted speaker with children, "Uncle Jim" quickly had their attention and numbers continued to grow during the week. The Mission made a lasting impression and many young lives were changed. The event is still fresh in some hearts and minds.

THE CATHEDRAL JUBILEE

In the Spring of 1951 Princess Elizabeth and Prince Philip came to Liverpool to open the magnificent Rankin Porch of the Cathedral. In the great Vesty Tower, standing proud three hundred and thirty-one feet above them, the highest and heaviest peal of bells in the world rang out over the city in joyous acclamation.

The Jubilee of the Cathedral was celebrated in July 1954 with a series of spectacular services arranged by Dean Dwelly, using music, colour and movement to the full. At one service, attended by the Lord Mayor and Corporation, a presentation was made to the Dean and Chapter of the *Civic Cross*, a magnificent processional cross to be borne aloft at the head of the Cathedral Choir. Its design is unusual, in that it has two arms symbolising the two parallel transepts of the Cathedral.

FREDERICK WILLIAM DILLISTONE

When Canon B. S. Bezzant, Chancellor of the Cathedral for twenty years, was appointed Dean of St Johns College, Cambridge, the Bishop invited Dr. F. W. Dillistone, Professor of Theology at the Episcopal College, Cambridge, Massachuesettes, to return to England and fill the vacant post. In 1955, when Dwelly retired from the Deanery, Dillistone was persuaded to take his place, though he did so somewhat reluctantly. (About the same time the celebrated Cathedral organist, Dr. Goss Custard, retired, and a young organist, Noel Rawsthorne, one of his students, was appointed in his stead). The new Dean was a man of wide experience, who had been a missionary in India, Professor of Theology at Wycliffe College, Toronto and Vice-Principal of London College of Divinity. He was an eminent writer and biblical scholar and the author of several important theological works. Gracious, warm-hearted and hospitable, the Dean was often seen welcoming visitors to the Cathedral with a friendly smile. He was a thoughtful preacher and a gifted expositor of Scripture. He strengthened the links between the Cathedral and the clergy, restored the Cathedral organ, initiated the Cathedral Music Club and built up the membership of the Friends and Builders of the Cathedral. He was not afraid to experiment and introduced a Communion Service in place of Matins on one Sunday in the month. The innovation aroused some dissent, but the congregation soon adapted and came to appreciate the monthly Sacrament. On one occasion the entire service was televised. It was the first time the Service of Holy Communion had been seen on TV, and afterwards it was reported to be "the most ambitious religious broadcast ever tackled, including the Coronation",[3] and brought in scores of letters of appreciation from viewers. Dillistone's religious broadcasts on the radio were also listened to with much interest by a large audience;

It was something of a disappointment to the Bishop when the Dean decided to move to Oxford on his appointment as Chaplain and Fellow of Oriel College. However, it was a move which gave Dillistone the opportunity to fulfil a long-felt desire to write a biography of Dr Charles Raven. It was largely through the Dean's ministry that the Diocese came to appreciate the Cathedral more and more as the spiritual home of "the Family of God".

PAROCHIAL WEEKENDS

The Bishop at heart was a true pastor and during his Episcopate he planned a number of visits to parishes for the purpose of encouraging both clergy and laity in their Christian ministry. He enjoyed nothing more than being back in a parish and being close to the people. He loved to see the laity usefully employed in Christian service, and he would ask "a home parish" to provide fifty helpers together with fifty helpers from "an away parish" to come together to do some house to house visiting.

On the Friday evening the Bishop met members of the Parochial Church Council and Church leaders quite informally to discuss with them any problems and share with them their plans for the future. On the Saturday afternoon, two or three teams of lay workers arrived from other parishes in the Diocese for a short commissioning service, before going out two by two with workers from "the home parish" to visit the surrounding houses. They left the church wondering what kind of reception they would receive and returned at the end of the afternoon overjoyed and having shared together in a wonderful experience. They invited parishioners to share in the weekend services with the Bishop and brought back useful information about the sick and homes where a follow-up might be useful.

Bishop Martin related easily to people and during his stay in the parish he listened intently to people, baptised, confirmed, preached, conducted a Family Service on Sunday afternoon and administered the Holy Communion to large congregations. Clergy and parishioners were delighted to have the Bishop and Mrs Martin spend time with them and they responded with enthusiasm.

An admirer of the Church of England's parochial system, the Bishop recognised the Church's responsibility for the spiritual and moral care of every man, woman and child in the parish. There were two hundred and thirty parishes in the Diocese served

MISSION

by three hundred and twenty-five clergy. He saw it as a great privilege for the clergy to have such a close contact with the people, especially at such important points in their lives as baptisms, weddings and funerals. The Bishop was delighted to learn that in the tenth year of his Episcopate records showed that there were no less than seven thousand candidates confirmed in the Diocese, including some four thousand confirmed at one service in the Cathedral.

DELEGATES TO THE STATES

In 1954 the Bishop and a small delegation from the Diocese attended the Anglican Congress in Minneapolis. There were six hundred and fifty-seven representatives attending from every quarter of the Anglican Communion. The debates, discussions and services enabled them all to discover and appreciate what it really means to belong to the worldwide Church. The report the delegates brought back moved the Diocese to extend its vision overseas and attempt to do more to meet the needs of the family of God abroad.

From Minneapolis the delegates went on to attend the Second Assembly of the World Council of Churches at Evanston, representing one hundred and sixty-three churches in forty eight countries. The message which came out of Evanston was relevant to the times: "To stay together is not enough, we must go forward". It was noticeable at the time that the churches in the Diocese were prepared to work closer together and demonstrate a growing measure of unity between them.

Again in August 1963 Martin and a party of delegates from the Diocese attended the Second Anglican Congress in Toronto, where the Bishop made some significant contributions to the debates and the delegates were inspired by accounts of the Church's Mission in the Third World. When they returned home, the delegates received an enthusiastic welcome at a crowded meeting in the Central Hall, who in turn were inspired and challenged by the Bishop's report on the visit to Canada.

MISSIONARY CONCERNS

The Diocese has always had a strong missionary interest and parishes have given generous support, prayerfully, financially and in personal service to the Church overseas. At the Diocesan Conferences and at missionary meetings, the Bishop encouraged parishes to deepen their knowledge of the worldwide Church and be even more concerned over the needs of the Church abroad.

When a student at Cambridge Martin had seriously considered offering himself to a missionary society for work overseas, but his health was not strong and he had to settle for work at home. It was a great joy to him as Youth Secretary of the Church Missionary Society to visit churches and youth clubs to present the claims of Christ and the challenge of the mission field.

Mrs Martin also took a keen interest in missionary work and was often invited to speak at CMS and other missionary gatherings in the Diocese. It was a great thrill to them both, when their daughter Ruth, was accepted as a missionary and went out under the auspices of CMS to Nigeria. The Bishop and Mrs Martin had the privilege and joy of seeing her at work in a missionary situation and on another occasion of staying with missionaries in the Sudan.

MISSION

For many years the Bishop was the energetic chairman of the Overseas Council of the Church Assembly, during which he did everything in his power to keep the vision of the Church abroad before the Church at home. It was a thrill for him to attend with Mrs Martin, the annual rallies of the CMS in the Philharmonic Hall, Liverpool, and to hear first hand reports of the triumphs of the Gospel on the mission field. One outstanding event was the Diocesan Missionary Festival in 1956 in the Floral Hall, Southport, when Bishop Stephen Neil, who was serving the Church in South India so devotedly, spoke of his work and the progress being made in Christian unity.

To mark the Seventy-Fifth Anniversary of the Diocese, the Bishop expressed the hope that seventy-five young men and women from the parishes, would dedicate their lives and offer themselves for full-time Christian service, either at home or overseas.

THE 75TH ANNIVERSARY

The Celebrations for the Anniversary were carefully planned over a year under Martin's chairmanship. The theme he chose for the Anniversary Year was appropriately, *The Family of God*. The Board of Finance published an illustrated magazine, which described in a popular style and with excellent black and white photographs, something of the life and work of *The Family of God* in the Diocese, and sold large numbers at 1/- per copy. The Bishop wrote the Foreword in which he said:" We aim to make this idea of family life in the Church much more evident ...in the parishes and in the wider life of the Church (and) it must always be our aim to win others into the Church and so extend the family". Under the Bishop's leadership the Diocese became more of a family of parishes, with the Cathedral as the Mother Church, and an occasional meeting place for the whole family of God. A former Dean said of Bishop Martin: "Officially the Visitor, he was in a very special way the friend of the Cathedral. And when he was present on Diocesan occasions, the Cathedral was indeed the Mother Church".[4]

The Festival Service took place in the Cathedral on June 11th to celebrate the founding of the Diocese in 1880. Every parish was invited to participate and send representatives and consequently every seat in the Cathedral was filled. Some retained vivid memories as children of Ryle's Enthronement Service in the pro-Cathedral and later the laying of the foundation stone of the new Cathedral and now they were witnessing another stage in the life and growth of this magnificent building. It was an inspired choice to invite Christopher Chavasse, the Bishop of Rochester, to preach the sermon at the Festival Service. He contributed to an impressive service with a passionate sermon on "The Church as the Family of God".

The next day Bishop Martin preached at the Centenary Service in the Cathedral to mark the founding of the *Liverpool Daily Post*, in which he gave thanks for "a respectable newspaper". He went on to draw a parallel between the Press and the Church; pointing out that both are concerned with communication, presented in a form which can be readily understood, and above all, with publishing the truth.

Anniversary Year was an occasion of great celebrations in the Diocese led by the

Bishop, who called on the people to give thanks and praise to God for the work and witness of the Church on Merseyside and to pray for his continued blessing on all their work.

REGINALD GEORGE LINDSAY

Canon Lindsay spent almost the whole of his ministry in Liverpool, except for eight years he worked as a missionary in Kowloon. On his return to the Diocese he was appointed vicar of St John's, Waterloo, before moving on to St Saviour's, Everton, and then St Cyprian's, Edge Hill. In his later years he did a fine work as vicar of St Michael's, Garston. He gave nearly sixty years to the work of ministry and was a faithful pastor, an inspired preacher and a wise counsellor.

Reg Lindsay was more than willing to take on a job for the Diocese and when he retired from the parochial ministry the Bishop asked if he would take over responsibility for organising the recently formulated Christian Stewardship Campaign. Stewardship Campaigns were a new initiative in the Church of England and when other dioceses set up the organisation, they generally appointed a paid administrator with an office and staff to run things, but Lindsay was quite happy to take on the job on a voluntary basis with a room and a part-time secretary in Church House.

He invited clergy, Christian businessmen, teachers and others to train as Campaign directors and arranged for them to address Church Councils and Campaign conferences, perhaps in the setting of an evening dinner, on the benefits of Stewardship. Over a decade or more he was responsible for organising sixty-nine campaigns, which challenged the standards of Christian giving in the parishes, gave an opportunity to the laity to bear a Christian witness by regular house to house visiting in their neighbourhood, and raised thousands of pounds by direct giving for the needs of the Diocese and work overseas.

IN PRAISE OF READERS

The admission of Lay Readers to the Church dates back to the middle of the last century and the Diocese has always valued the willingness of the laity to actively support the clergy in their ministry. In 1957 there were two hundred Readers serving in the parishes, but numbers were gradually falling and Martin drew attention to the splendid work carried out by both Diocesan and Parochial Readers in so many parishes, and urged Christian laymen to consider training as Readers. Readership is an honorary office and to qualify candidates sat an examination on Bible and Prayer Book knowledge and took a test in reading clearly and distinctly. Successful applicants were admitted as Readers by the Bishop at a special service in the Cathedral or a Parish Church.

Martin was anxious to increase the number of Readers and he set out clearly in the Diocesan Leaflet the kind of work involved in this ministry. He classified the main duties as assisting the clergy in the Sunday services and occasionally preaching, teaching in the Sunday School and undertaking leadership of the Youth Work. Sometimes, if a vicar requested, the Bishop might authorise a Reader in a busy parish to administer the chalice at the Communion Service. During the interregnum between a change of clergy the Reader often did a very useful job by filling the gap

MISSION

in the ministry and helping to keep things "ticking-over" until the new man arrived. A survey carried out in 1967 revealed that on any one Sunday as many as seventy-five sermons were preached by Readers in the Diocese and they assisted at one hundred and eighty-nine services. The Bishop's telling appeal persuaded some to go forward and the clergy reported that several fine Christian laymen were prayerfully considering the possibility of becoming Readers.

ST HELENS DEANERY

St Helens situated in the centre of the Diocese grew out of the Industrial Revolution and developed rapidly after the arrival of the railway in the second quarter of the nineteenth century. The surrounding area was part of the Lancashire coal mining industry and in addition to mining the community relied for a living on the production of glass and chemicals, alkali and copper smelting and engineering.

St Helen, the Parish Church in the town centre, was the first church in the Diocese to be consecrated by Bishop David after a fire had destroyed the former church. Originally the ancient chapel of St Elyn or St Helen, the church earlier in the century was known as St Mary's. The new church built of red brick with a massive Gothic tower cost £80,000. The parish church has always had a strong evangelical tradition and this tradition influenced the ministry of several new churches in the area built to meet the demands of a growing population. A notable characteristic of St Helens churches was the Sunday afternoon Bible Class. It was not just for youngsters, but separate classes of men and women. The first classes were established at the parish church in 1888 when there were two thousand names on the books with an average attendance of five hundred. At the Diamond Jubilee in 1948, many former class members, some of whom had left the town, were delighted to return for the occasion, to meet old friends and to reminisce. During the 1930s there was much unemployment in the town and J. G. Tiarks (1937-1944) is remembered for the sterling work he did at that time, He became Provost of Bradford Cathedral in 1944 and was consecrated Bishop of Chelmsford in 1962. He was succeeded by R. B. Bailey (1944-1960) and then K. W. Coates (1960-1988).

St Luke's. Eccleston, was opened in 1910 as a Conventional District with a curate-in-charge. On 20 June 1931 a new church was consecrated by Bishop H. Gresford Jones, and F. H. Milward (1931-1939) was instituted and inducted the first vicar. In 1956 the parish published an attractive brochure celebrating the 25th Anniversary of the church and parish. The vicar, L. R. Barker (1955-1963), invited past vicars and curates to return to the parish and preach at the special Sunday services during June and July, concluding with a visit by Bishop Martin. Among the preachers were Hugh Jordan (1939-1946), J. G. Williams (1946-1951), and D. C. Moore (1951-1955). When Barker left the parish he was succeeded by S. T. Lane (1963-1971). It is interesting to note that at one time the organ in St Luke's once belonged to the Beecham family and stood for many years in their works in the town. One of the great events in the life of the parish at this time was the Annual Procession of Witness and Field Day on August Bank Holiday Monday, when parishioners enjoyed a fun day of sports, stalls and refreshments on a local field.

MISSION

St Peter's. Parr, built in 1865, a year after the first church was destroyed by fire, was originally a daughter church of Prescot Parish Church and became a separate parish in 1845. For the Centenary the parish published a Centenary Brochure with a description of the opening of the new church and an interesting account of the ministry of A. A. Nunn, a gifted Irishman, who was vicar of the parish for over forty years and responsible for the church being built on a new site after a disastrous fire destroyed the earlier church. During the period under review the clergy were A. V. Diamond (1936-1949), F. L. Jones (1949-1956) and A. S. Thorne (1957-1970). St Peter's served a population of 2,000 when first built, but over the years it has grown until it is now estimated that some 35,000 live in the parish.

St James', Eccleston Park, was opened in 1923 to minister to a growing residential district on the edge of St Helens. It was a dual-purpose building serving as a place of worship on Sundays and a hive of activity during the rest of the week. Among the organisations which used the hall regularly were the Church of England Men's Society, the Mothers' Union and the "Seekers Club" for young people. In July 1961 St James' became a separate parish and Bishop Martin instituted I. L. Davies, who had served for two years as curate-in-charge, as the first vicar (1959-1970). Among the clergy who had previously served as curate-in-charge of the mission church attached to Christ Church, Eccleston, were W. Watson (1947-1953) and A. A. de Gruyther (1953-1959).

In 1962 the parish published a Review booklet analysing the day to day running expenses of the church as a challenge to Christians to give generously to the parish's direct giving scheme. The parish had an active Sunday School and Bible Class, uniformed movements for the young people and a pastoral committee to keep abreast of parish needs. The "Eight-Five Special" on Sunday evenings catered for young people and was well supported.

The present church of St Matthew, Thatto Heath, replacing an earlier church, was consecrated by the Bishop of Warrington on 27 July 1954. Originally a daughter church of Christ Church, Eccleston, and opened in 1917, it served a rapidly growing area. At the end of the War the members started planning and saving to build a new church and raised £3.500 through the Brick Fund. Eventually the total cost of £30.000 was met partly through a generous allocation from the Diocesan Church Aid Fund, a grant from the War Damages Fund, and a loan of £10.000 from the Diocese. The Bishop in his sermon warmly thanked the Mayor and members of the Borough Council for their interest in the work of the Church in St Helens, and congratulated the church members on their achievement in building a new parish church within such a short time. The first vicar was S. G. Ogden (1948-1955). who had already served seven years as curate-in-charge of the Conventional District. More than average numbers attended the services on the first Sunday, and the vicar arranged a special Family Service in the afternoon when he explained the significance of the various items within the church, the font, the lectern, the holy table and the pulpit. When Ogden left he was succeeded by a local clergyman, F. A. Dean (1955-1964) and then A. Rhodes (1964-1967).

FAREWELL

For sometime the Bishop had felt that he was beginning to slow down and his thoughts turned toward retirement. He had been a devoted Father in God in the Diocese for twenty-one years and he quietly announced that he had decided to pass the work on to another at the end of November 1965. It was a special joy to him before leaving Liverpool to lead a party in pilgrimage to the Holy Land.

Laurence Brown, who had succeeded Robert Claxton as the Bishop of Warrington, together with a group of helpers, arranged the Bishop's Farewell Gathering in the Central Hall, which was attended by representatives of the council, commerce and church. Wellwishers spoke of the Bishop's faithful, unselfish and inspiring leadership, the ever-open door at Bishop's Lodge, the joy and fellowship of the Swanwick and Blackpool Conferences, and how appropriate it was that the Farewell should be held in the Methodist Central Hall, since the Bishop had worked ceaselessly to bring about closer relations between Church and Chapel.

After the presentations to the Bishop and Mrs Martin, the Bishop said they planned to move into a bungalow near Evesham in Worcestershire and he hoped to purchase a small Morris 1100 to get around in.

Before he left the Diocese the University made him an honorary Doctor of Law in recognition of his outstanding work and he was overjoyed to become a Fellow of St Peter's College, Oxford. But the crowning moment was, undoubtedly, the Communion Service in the Cathedral on the evening of St Andrew's Day. It was a most memorable service on an appropriate day, sensitively arranged by the Dean, Edward Patey, who had arrived in the Diocese only the year before. It was the last time the Bishop preached and celebrated the Sacrament in the Cathedral and everyone sensed it was truly the *Family of God* gathered to bid farewell to a greatly-loved *Father in God.*

Mrs Martin did not enjoy the best of health in later years and died after a long illness in 1972. The Bishop survived his wife by five years and died shortly before his eighty-second birthday.

Bishop Martin came to the Diocese at a difficult time toward the end of the Second World War during which Liverpool and Merseyside had suffered so much loss and damage. The Diocese had generously supported the Bishop's *Call to Build Fund* to rebuild and restore the War damaged churches and erect new churches and parochial halls on the new housing estates. Martin was at heart an evangelist and pastor and the long week-ends he spent in the parishes, preaching and teaching, were never forgotten. He longed to see a renewal and revival of spiritual life in the parishes, the laity more involved in the work of the Church and a closer co-operation with other churches in the work of evangelism.

Chapter 6

EDIFICATION

The 1960s was an exciting time. Britain had thrown off the post-War depression and there was an air of confidence in the future It was the era of the Permissive Society, which gave rise to an entirely new culture. Overnight young people became "Hippies". Youths with shoulder-length hair wore jeans and multi-coloured shirts and ties, and girls dressed in miniskirts. It was the "Swinging Sixties". "Rock and roll" had arrived from America and night after night the "Cavern" in Liverpool was crowded with hysterical fans of the Beatles.

The Council had an energetic scheme of building new houses and especially high-rise blocks of flats on open spaces within the city and farmland out in the suburbs. Over thirty thousand slum properties had been declared inhabitable in the city and left a huge waiting list for new homes. The Council decided that tower-blocks, some eleven or more stories high, would be the cheapest and quickest way of housing the many needy families. The creation of these new blocks of flats changed the skyline of Liverpool and the new towns of Kirkby and Skelmersdale.

STUART YARWORTH BLANCH

After leaving school Stuart Blanch worked in the insurance business until the out-break of War and he was called up. He enlisted in the RAF and trained at a huge camp on Heaton Park, Manchester. He became a corporal with the RAF Police before transferring to Transport Command as a navigator. His duties took him to many scenes of operation, including India and Canada.

It was during his service in the Royal Air Force that he was converted to Christ. He became a Christian, not through a chaplain or a church service, but simply by thoughtfully reading his Bible during, as he said, a slack period on guard duty at the camp. From that day on he developed a great love for the Scriptures, together with an appreciation of the privilege of prayer and a burning desire to share his faith with others.

About the same time, a pretty young woman, Brenda Gertrude Coyte, also became a Christian, and sometime later when their paths crossed, they fell in love and decided to get married.

At the end of the War, believing that God was calling him into the Christian ministry, Blanch went up to Oxford to take his degree and then on to Wycliffe Hall to study theology. He was no mean scholar and left University with first class honours, and was ordained to a curacy at All Saint's, Highgate, Oxford. After three years he moved on to the benefice of Eynsham, a country parish a few miles out of Oxford. It was a big jump from wearing a uniform to putting on a cassock and surplice.

EDIFICATION

Someone who knew him well, commented that he was "a layman in holy orders, surprised to find that God had put him there".[1]

Brenda often recalled those early day of married life in a parish. They had three children when her husband was still a curate, and she once told listeners on local radio: "I used to pack them all into a pram, tie the dog to the handle, and take them everywhere with me. When the fifth arrived Stuart used to bathe the other four while I was feeding the baby".

Blanch never lost touch with Oxford and after a worthwhile ministry in two parishes he was invited to return to Wycliffe Hall, his theological college, as Vice-Principal. The quality of his work with students was widely acknowledged and in 1960 he was appointed Warden of Rochester Theological College and Canon of Rochester Cathedral.

Six years later he was astonished to receive an important letter enquiring if he would be interested in his name going forward as the next Bishop of Liverpool. He never had the slightest ambition of ever occupying such an elevated position in the Church, and only after much prayer and with some trepidation, he agreed and was selected. Dr Habgood, when Archbishop of York, said of him, "He was surprised at finding himself ordained and surprised at being called to Liverpool."[2]

Though virtually unknown in the north of England, except by those fortunate ordinands, who had sat in on his interesting lectures, his nomination to Liverpool was received with great pleasure and the Diocese gave him a characteristically warm welcome.

Stuart Blanch was consecrated on the 25 March 1966 in York Minster by Donald Coggan, the Archbishop of York, in the presence of twenty-eight other bishops, civic representatives and a large congregation of clergy and laity, many of whom had travelled over from Liverpool and from as far away as Rochester. The sermon was preached by Canon G. T. Rogers, the Canon Missioner of Coventry, who took as his text: "If any man desire the office of a bishop, he desires a good work" (I Timothy 3: 1). He pointed out that times have changed and the work of a bishop has now become so arduous that few desire it. Certainly, Blanch had no wish to be made a bishop, but he felt sure he had been called and commissioned by God and he must obey.

PASTORAL OVERSIGHT

In all his ministry Stuart Blanch was a true pastor and under his leadership the Diocese continued to give priority to the spiritual and social needs of society. He was "a people's bishop" and one of the first tasks he set himself was to visit the inner city areas and the housing estates which were springing up in the new towns. He was a man of sound judgment and from this first-hand survey he was able to see for himself the quality of life (or lack of it) in some northern parishes. He now felt it important to appoint a planning office to expedite pastoral reorganisation and future projects.

He aimed to get to know all his clergy and their families and in his conversations

EDIFICATION

with both clergy and laity he quickly won their confidence by his friendliness, humanity and spirituality. He had a sound wisdom, a ready wit and a deep personal faith. His friendly smile endeared him to the people, and he soon had the affection and good-will of everyone in the Diocese.

TWO BISHOPS OF WARRINGTON

On coming to the Diocese the Bishop was delighted to have the friendship, guidance and support of Laurence Brown, the Bishop of Warrington, for the past five years. Brown had been the Archdeacon of Lewisham and Canon Residentiary of Southwark Cathedral in 1960 when he received the invitation to become a Suffragan Bishop. He was able to share his knowledge of the Diocese with Stuart on his arrival in Liverpool and together they formed a close-working relationship during the next three years. He had a passionate interest in the creation and support of churches on the new estates and was a hearty supporter of the Bishop's *Call to Build Fund*. Among the things he enjoyed was the growing relationship between the different traditions in the Church and the experiments in sharing churches. He also took a particular interest in the Mersey Mission to Seamen and often visited with the Mission Chaplain the Bar Lightship in Liverpool Bay. In 1969 he was translated to the See of Birmingham.

The following year the Bishop nominated Canon John Monier Bickersteth, the vicar of St Stephen's, Rochester, his Suffragan Bishop. Educated at Rugby and Christ Church, Oxford, he was during the War a captain in the Buffs and the Royal Artillery. An enthusiastic bishop, he also took a special interest in urban ministry and the planting of churches on the new estates. He also became deeply involved with housing problems and the improvement of industrial relations on Merseyside.

However, after only five years in the Diocese he was translated to the See of Bath and Wells. For him it was a return to familiar ground for had been trained for the Ministry at Wells Theological College, and had served on Dr Mervyn Stockwood's staff at St Matthew's, Bristol. His new Diocese in contrast to Liverpool was mainly rural, served by some two hundred country churches.

EDWARD HENRY PATEY

The new Dean of Liverpool came from Coventry Cathedral in 1964. For the past six years he had been a Canon Residentiary, working chiefly among young people and helping to produce with great flair some experimental multi-racial and multi-denominational services.

He was an enthusiastic in all his work, a radical thinker, a masterly organiser and a gifted preacher, whose sole desire in his ministry was to make the gospel of Jesus Christ known to the modem world.

When he took up his appointment he introduced several Worship Celebrations, involving music, dance and drama, and the Cathedral soon became known as "Patey's Pavilion" On one occasion, he attracted a vast congregation of teenagers by inviting the pop group, the Bee Gees, to perform in the centre space of the Cathedral.

EDIFICATION

Some of his innovations roused a great deal of criticism, which was picked up by the press and simmered for several weeks. He was severely criticised when young people were seen jiving in the central space of the Cathedral. But gradually it was recognised that new ways had to be tried if the younger generation was to be reached with the gospel. He insisted that "there must be continual experiment if Cathedral worship is not to become a mere fossilisation of the past, a museum piece, an antiquarian hangover".[3] On another occasion, he was severely criticised, for quite a different reason, when he invited Augustine Harris, the Catholic Auxiliary Bishop of Liverpool, to occupy the Cathedral pulpit.

THE UNFINISHED CATHEDRAL

A dilemma facing Patey on his arrive in Liverpool was whether work on the Cathedral should be completed or postponed until a later date when money might be more readily available. The massive structure was only two thirds complete and funds were running low. The question was, "Should the Cathedral be finished as planned, and if so, where was the money to come from?" It had been evident to the Cathedral Chapter for some time that "as the building rose higher and higher, so did its costs".[4] There were many critics in Liverpool and throughout the country who insisted that the Cathedral was large enough to meet modern needs and no more money should be ploughed into the project. Voices were raised against the "Liverpool Folly" and the *Liverpool Daily Post and Echo* gave considerable space to these opinions and the Cathedral committee had to take the objections seriously. There were many other needs demanding support in the Diocese and particularly overseas. After many long discussions and much heart-searching, it was eventually agreed that the Cathedral should be completed as planned and in May 1968 the committee, with the Bishop's backing, hopefully launched the *Finish The Cathedral Appeal*.

Patey justified the decision in a statement to the press, saying, 'Liverpool Cathedral is probably used and appreciated by as large a section of the community as any cathedral in the country... Your leader writer should have been here when over 4,000 children thronged the cathedral in a thrilling and dramatic act of worship to welcome the new bishop, when over 3,0000 young people took part in a Christmas service which really spoke in their language about the meaning of the Incarnation; or when just recently over 2,000 husbands and wives were deeply moved in a service: *In Praise of Marriage'*.[5]

The Cathedral Appeal met with an excellent response and the target of raising £500,000 within seven years was speedily reached and work on the building went ahead. Following the death of Sir Giles Scott, the creative genius, who had given so much of his life to planning the Cathedral, it was left to Frederick Thomas, the associate architect, to design and finish the West Front. Without slavishly following Scott's ideas, the blue-print he set before the committee was in perfect harmony with the earlier style of the Cathedral.

There was still much work to be done and it was a further twenty years before the building was completed. Inflation and rising costs after the War meant, as the Dean pointed out, that the final phase "cost nearly as much as all the work which has been done to that time".[6]

CALL TO THE NORTH

The Call to the North Campaign in the beginning was an initiative of Stuart Blanch who desired to see the churches working closer together in making known the good news of the gospel and was later taken up by Dr Coggan, the Archbishop of York, in the northern Province. In Liverpool Diocese the actual "Call" took the form of a joint pastoral letter sent out to all the churches from Stuart Blanch, Andrew Beck, the Roman Catholic Archbishop, and Dr John Marsh, Moderator of the Free Church Federal Council. It asked for a year of prayer and learning in preparation for some specific acts of Christian witness during Holy Week 1973 and aimed to draw together the various denominations in partnership. It was primarily an evangelistic effort, but unusual in that it did not follow a tradition pattern but was a combination of spiritual and social activities. The laity played their part in visiting the homes in the participating parishes and the response was encouraging. One lasting result was that it laid the foundation for future ecumenical co-operation between the churches. and all the leaders of the main denominations continued to meet afterwards on a regular basis to promote further avenues of united service.

THE METROPOLITAN CATHEDRAL

The Roman Catholic Archdiocese of Liverpool established in 1850 did not have a Cathedral until more recent times. Work began in 1933 on building which was planned to have a dome larger that St Peter's in Rome, but only the crypt was finished.

The completed Catholic Cathedral of Christ the King in Liverpool was consecrated by Archbishop George Beck on the Feast of Pentecost 1967. The Catholic Cathedral stands in marked contrast to the Anglican Cathedral, being very modern in style and constructed entirely of steel, concrete and glass. The tent-like structure, surmounted by a magnificent lantern of coloured glass, is symbolic of Jesus' crown of thorns. The circular form of the Cathedral lends itself to worship "in the round" allowing all to participate round the central altar. The Cathedral has affectionately become known to all Liverpudlians as "Paddy's Wigwam" or "The Mersey Funnel" and is greatly admired.

The service of Consecration was witnessed by thousands on television and attended by the Bishops of Liverpool and Warrington with Dean Patey, representing the Diocese. To mark the occasion the Dean and Chapter commissioned a music score, *In cantatias*, which was performed at the service by Noel Rawsthorne, organist of the Anglican Cathedral.

A GROWING UNITY

There were few signs of "anti-popery" feeling in the city or outside the

EDIFICATION

Metropolitan Cathedral on the day of the Consecration. In the post-War years, relations between the Anglican and Catholic hierarchy had grown closer and there is less animosity and a greater feeling of tolerance at grass-roots level. At a United Service in April 1967 the Auxiliary Bishop of Liverpool, Augustine Harris, was the first Roman Catholic to preach in the Anglican Cathedral. A few years later Archbishop Beck preached at an inaugural service in the Cathedral at the beginning of an ecumenical conference on *Confessing Christ together today*. When Bishop Blanch moved in to Bishop's Lodge in Woolton the first telegram he received was from Archbishop Beck who lived almost opposite. The Bishop and the Archbishop cemented the good relations between the two Churches, and the Archbishop was personally invited to attend the Bishop's last Eucharist celebrated in the Cathedral before his translation to York. It was the first time the Archbishop had attended a Communion Service in an Anglican Church.

Old prejudices die hard and at an Ecumenical Service in the Cathedral early in 1970, seventy-five protesters interrupted Cardinal Willabrands, president of the Vatican Secretariat for Christian Unity, when he began to preach, by shouting and waving "No Popery" banners and the police had to be called to eject them. Unfortunately, one of the demonstrators suffered a heart-attack in all the commotion and died on his way to hospital.

Ever since official talks began in 1955 between the Anglican and Methodist Churches there has been a growing hope that the two denominations would draw closer together. In 1965 plans were drawn up for a reunion to take place in two stages between the two Churches and when the vote was taken the Methodists were in full agreement, but not the Anglicans and the scheme was shelved. Stuart longed to see the two Churches in the Diocese working together in harmony and in 1971 he organised an Anglican-Methodist Synod, at which obstacles to union were openly discussed and ways forward were explored. A year later the Congregationalists and English Presbyterians came together to form the United Reformed Church, and expectations were raised that Anglicans would agree to uniting with the Methodists, but for a second time, the proposal was rejected. The Bishop and many in the Diocese were bitterly disappointed and decided to strengthen the ties between the two Churches on a local level. The Merseyside Christian Ecumenical Council and local Councils of Christian Churches worked more closely together as a result.

THE NORTH WEST ORDINATION COURSE

In Rochester Stuart Blanch had had a successful ministry in teaching and training mature students for the Anglican ministry and when he observed that the number of clergy in the Diocese was gradually falling and parishes were failing to challenge Christian young men to consider the Christian ministry as a vocation, he wrote several articles in the *Liverpool Diocesan News* on the need for dedicated Christian laity to train for the ministry.

For some time the Church of England had been considering closing some of the Theological Colleges since the flow of ordinands into the ministry was drying up. It

EDIFICATION

happened that one of the Colleges selected for closure was St Aidan's Theological College, Birkenhead. After sixty years of service to the Church it was decided that the College should be closed, or possibly be amalgamated with Hartley Victoria Methodist College, Manchester. During those sixty years St Aidan's had trained hundreds of ordinands and provided the north-west, in particular, with many hard-working parish clergy.

With the virtual demise of the College, Stuart saw an opportunity for a forward movement in theological training and he became a leading advocate in setting-up the NorthWest Regional Training Scheme. He favoured the overseas pattern in which ordinands from different traditions "trained together and learned to share each others riches".[7] He believed that Christian unity was a duty and not simply an option, and was delighted when the new "united College" was opened. The College welcomes students of both sexes from the Dioceses of Manchester, Chester, Blackburn, Wakefield, Lichfield and Liverpool, and from the other main denominations of the Church. In 1969 some forty-three students had enrolled for the three-year part-time course of weekly lectures and seminars with occasional week-end residential courses. There were those who thought the scheme was doomed to fail, but it continues to meet a wide need and many parishes are grateful for the clerical assistance the new College has provided.

Many of those who have been trained at the College and ordained are Non-Stipendiary Ministers, a new category of minister in the modern Church. NSMs continue in their secular employment during the week and assist in the parishes mainly at the week-end. They are not "second-class priests", nor simply "ministers on the cheap", but over the years they have given invaluable service in many parishes, which would have have been in dire straits without their assistance.

SWANWICK CONFERENCES

The Annual Conference was well established when Stuart arrived in the Diocese and he was enthusiastic about its continuance and expansion. Parishes were encouraged to send representatives from the Parochial Church Council and Organisations to meet in pleasant surroundings in Derbyshire to discuss in Christian fellowship important issues affecting the life of the Church, and then to report back to their own Church Councils. In June 1967 over two hundred delegates considered *What the Bible says about Ministry in the Twentieth Century* and returned to their parishes with a fresh vision of the Church's work and commissioned to keep every PCC regularly informed about forward steps in Ministry.

The following year the theme chosen was *Preaching the Gospel in the Twentieth Century*, and again, the Conference Centre at Swanwick attracted a large number, including for the first time, representatives from the Methodist Church. After much prayerful discussion the Conference concluded that the Christian message must be preached in relevant terms which could be understood by the man in the street; that the clergy should not be left to do everything in the parish, and the laity should take a greater responsibility for evangelism in partnership with Christians from other churches in the neighbourhood.

EDIFICATION

HALEWOOD ECUMENICAL CHURCH

As early as 1964 the Anglicans and Methodists had discussed the possibility of a united church on a large housing estate in Halewood. There were few difficulties to overcome and within a short time members of the two Churches began visiting and winning the support of the people on the estate for a united church. A year later a magazine was published giving more details of the project and interest began to grow. Then the leaders of both denominations took a step of faith and work began on building an ecumenical church in the parish. Through the Bishop's *Call to Build Fund*, the Anglicans promised to contribute £400 per annum over ten years toward the cost of building and the endowment of the new church.

There were great celebrations on 11 March 1967 when Bishop Blanch dedicated the new combined Anglican-Methodist Church at Halewood in the presence of a full congregation of enthusiastic Christians united in a new venture. The building was due in no small measure to the amiable relationship between the Rector and the Methodist Minister working together in unison in evangelizing and building-up from a small beginning the body of Christ on this large estate.

Sadly the church was destroyed by fire in 1972, but the members rallied together and were determined to raise a new church out of the ashes and within a little more than a year their aim was fulfiled. The church in the past two decades has grown together and holds joint services including Communion under the leadership of a team ministry of a Team Rector, a Team Vicar, a Methodist Minister and a Non Stipendiary Minister.

A similar pattern of joint ministry is also working in Skelmersdale at the Church in the Centre; at St Philip's, Westbrook, and Trinity Church, Roby.

THE DIOCESAN SYNOD

Under the Synodical Government Measure 1969, a Diocesan Synod was established in every Diocese replacing the Diocesan Conference. The old Diocesan Conference, first called together by Ryle, had witnessed many rousing debates and made many important decisions and the last one was held in 1970. The Synod works on three levels: National, Diocesan and Deanery and is intended to allow bishops, clergy and laity to share views in open discussion on important issues before the Church. Like the General Synod, the Diocesan Synod has three "Houses" - Bishops, Clergy and Laity. The clergy and laity are elected by the deanery synod and generally serve for five years. The first Synod, a much smaller body than the Conference, met in 1971 in St Katherine's College. Synod continues to discuss the familiar subjects of Finance, Church Buildings, Education and Social Responsibilities along with contemporary issues It is said to be a more democratic and efficient body, but some consider the old order was better when clergy and laity were directly involved in the discussions rather than through proxies in cabinet.

NEW CHURCHES ON NEW ESTATES

St Mark's, Dallam, was dedicated on 9 September 1954 to serve the people who

EDIFICATION

had moved into the new houses on Dallam Farm estate. Before the church was erected the congregation used to meet for worship in the School Hall in the village. Once a farming community St Mark's now ministers to families employed in a variety of trades and professions in and around Warrington. The dual-purpose building with the addition of an extension at the rear was used for various activities during the week and for well-attended services on Sundays. Among the clergy who have served as curate-in-charge at St Mark's are D. G. A. Bennett (1963-1969), J. C. Rimmer (1969-1974) and I. Elliott (1974-1983). St Mark's was created a new parish in 1980.

St Mark's, Childwall Valley, began from a small beginning in the 1960s, when All Saint's, Childwall, designated a curate to move on to the estate and build up a congregation. After the laborious work of "ploughing" and "sowing" in "church planting" had been completed, it was agreed that a daughter-church with a curate's house should be built on the estate, and residents were asked to "Buy a Brick" for the new building at 10p each. The foundation stone of the new church was laid by Bishop Blanch in July 1973 and dedicated by him on 31 March the following year. On the following Sunday the Rev. R. Johnson (1972-1976), who had succeeded A. Siddal (1970-1972) as minister-in-charge, administered Holy Communion, baptised nine infants and preached to packed congregations. St Marks became one of the three churches within the Gateacre Team Ministry, along with St Stephen's and Christ Church, Netherley.

When St Chad's, the parish church of Kirkby, was consecrated by the Bishop of Chester in 1871, replacing the earlier church of 1766, the vicar had eight-curates to assist him in his large rural parish. Immediately after the War, Liverpool Corporation had plans for developing the area and rehousing in Kirkby many of those whose homes had been destroyed in the Blitz or condemned as unfit for human habitation. By 1959 fifty thousand inhabitants lived on the estates in the new town in private and local authority houses. In 1961 the Urban District Council developed the Civic Centre in the town centre and opened the 10,000th house on the estate. The nearby industrial estates provided employment for large numbers at this time until the economic situation worsened in the early 1970s and the community has never fully recovered.

In the 1960s J. A. Lawton was the incumbent at St Chad's and when the Bishop appointed him Archdeacon of Warrington he was succeeded in 1969 by J. Waine, the vicar of Holy Trinity, Southport. The parish was among the first in the Diocese in 1971 to become a Team Ministry, under the pastoral reorgan;sation of the parishes. It was a team of seven clergy. In time, three new churches were dedicated in strategic areas of the parish, St Martin's (1964), St Mark's (1970), and St Andrew's (1976). Waine remained Team Rector until 1975, when he was appointed Suffragan Bishop of Stafford. Among those clergy who served in the parish as Team Vicars were T. A. Gibson, who became Team Rector on Waine's departure; R. Lewis, who became Domestic Chaplain to the Archbishop of York in 1975; G. I Hurst (1971-1975) and C. M. Smith (1974-1981).

EDIFICATION

ARCHBISHOP OF YORK

There were mixed feelings in the Diocese when it was announced that the Bishop had been appointed to succeed Dr Coggan as Archbishop. Preaching in the Cathedral he said he clearly remembered the morning when the postman delivered a letter to him from Harold Wilson, the Prime Minister: "It came in one of those plain white envelopes that you open with caution. I am only now beginning to get over the shock". Dr John Habgood, later Archbishop of York, in paying tribute to his predecessor, said of him: "His surprise originated, not from any lack of gifts to do the work entrusted to him, but from a deep sense of himself as a simple ordinary Christian, who studied his Bible and loved his Lord and had no relish for ecclesiastical pomp - and still less for ecclesiastical politics".[8] The Archbishop-elect admitted that he was "not well up in central church administration" and realised that going to York would be a tough job so there was need for much prayer.

In Liverpool Stuart Blanch was well liked by everyone whether or not they were churchgoers, It was widely recognised that he was an able leader with a deep spirituality and much common sense, but it was not expected that he would be leaving after so short a time. A consolation was that he would not be lost entirely to the Diocese since his oversight of the Northern Province would mean a return to Liverpool from time to time.

The Bishop considered it a great challenge to follow Dr Coggan at York and he rejoiced to have the support of Brenda beside him and the good wishes of his family, In an interview on local radio before leaving the Diocese, Brenda said they would miss the warmth and friendship of the people of Liverpool and asked for their prayers as Stuart took up his new responsibilities in York.

On a Wednesday evening early in January 1975 a congregation of two thousand from all parts of the Diocese filled the Cathedral for a Farewell Communion Service at which the Bishop preached a simple, but inspiring and challenging message. He left the Diocese, he said, with two great thoughts, the friendliness and goodwill of the people and "a developing awareness that I have a man-size job on my hands and only God can save me". He left with the prayers and good wishes of the whole Diocese.

Under Stuart Blanch's leadership the Diocese had made great strides toward completing the work on the Cathedral, developing closer relations with other churches, and encouraging a more effective evangelistic and pastoral ministry in the parishes. He was a gifted teacher and left the Diocese with a better understanding of the Christian Faith. He gave unstinting support to his clergy and as "the layman's bishop", he urged the laity to take on more responsibilities in Christian service.

Chapter 7

RECONCILIATION

The year 1975 was a year of new beginnings in the Church of England. There was a recently installed Archbishop of Canterbury, Donald Coggan; a new Archbishop of York, Stuart Blanch, and a new Bishop of Liverpool, David Sheppard. In Liverpool some long established businesses were compelled to close down because of the slow-down in trade, unemployment rose sharply and there was frustration and anger in the Council over the lack of Government help. Many of those who had happily moved into new homes on green-field sites now felt trapped in high-rise blocks of flats with broken lifts, long dark corridors, noisy neighbours and problem families. Above all, they missed the close-knit community of the old neighbourhoods, where everyone knew their neighbours and where there was always a cheery word and a helping hand.

DAVID STUART SHEPPARD

David Sheppard was educated at Sherborne School, and after completing his National Service he went to Trinity Hall, Cambridge to study for his degree. It was while he was at Cambridge that a friend invited him to attend a church service which touched a nerve and that evening in his digs he prayed, asking Christ to take charge of his life as Saviour and Lord. After taking his degree he moved on to Ridley Hall to study theology, believing that God wanted him in the ministry. He was ordained in 1955 and for the next two years served as curate at St Mary's, Islington, a well-known evangelical church in north London.

David Sheppard has always had a love of cricket. In the Varsity Match against Oxford in 1951 he captained the side and knocked up 127 runs. Later he played regularly for Sussex and was a popular captain. He played in twenty-two Tests against the West Indies, Pakistan, India, Australia, and New Zealand. Twice he scored a century against Australia and once against India. He had the distinction of being the first parson to be selected to play in a Test Match. He continued to play for Sussex in several county matches until 1961 and in that year he played in the Gentlemen v Players match at Lords. In one game Sheppard dropped a very difficult catch, and quick as a flash, Fred Truman, in a strong Yorkshire accent, commented, "It is a pity Reverend don't put his hands together more often in t'field".[1]

At the end of his curacy Sheppard went to Canning Town as Warden of the Mayfair Family Centre, to continue a ministry of worship, evangelism and social service.

David and Grace, a clergyman's daughter, had only recently married and the work at the Centre was to be a new challenge to both of them. For twelve years they lived and worked together in a missionary situation. Surrounded day by day poverty, unemployment and depression, they continued to trust in the Lord and through much

RECONCILIATION

prayer they sought to bring hope to the people and ease their burdens. From small beginnings the work gradually produced results and became established.

David's caring and winsome ministry among an impoverished underclass was noticed by the Church hierarchy and in 1969 he was invited to become the Suffragan Bishop of Woolwich. He was forty years of age and the Church's youngest bishop. It was a time when the new towns were developing and the government was encouraging firms to move out from the old boroughs into the new regional development areas. The new buildings and surroundings were more pleasant places to work in, but the upheaval left behind thousands of redundant workers who had little hope of ever getting other jobs. This was the situation the bishop had to face and he recognised that it required a radical reappraisal. His priority was to proclaim the good news of the Gospel, but in doing so he could not ignore the desperate situation of the disadvantaged. He believed the message of the prophets should be heard again. The Christian faith had to be made visible in Christian action and he sought to show the love of God in his care and concern for the less fortunate. It was a wrench when he was pressed to leave his task unfinished in London and fill the vacant place in the See of Liverpool. There was so much more to do in Southwark, yet he saw it as a great challenge to take up the work as the chief pastor in an industrial Diocese in the north-west. He was installed the sixth Bishop of Liverpool in the Cathedral on St Barnabas Day, 11 June 1975, the day on which, almost a century before, the first Bishop of Liverpool had been consecrated.

David Sheppard is a man of deep Christian faith which stems from his undergraduate days and though he has opened his mind to some of the wider aspects of faith and practice in the Church, at heart he remains a evangelical with a deep love and trust in the Saviour and a burning desire to make known the gospel of Jesus Christ in all its richness. He would not presume to call himself a great theologian, but he is a very practical Bishop who believes that Christianity should be expressed clearly by the spoken and written word and in positive Christian action.

In modern times bishops are no longer prelates who live in palaces, and several years ago the Bishop of Liverpool ceased to live in the Bishop's Palace on Abercromby Square and moved to Bishop's Lodge in Woolton. This has become an open house for many informal gatherings of clergy and laity in the Diocese. Everyone who knows Bishop David is aware of his absolute sincerity and modesty, his enthusiasm and warm friendship. Grace Sheppard, too, soon won the hearts of the Diocese and, in addition to her own Christian ministry in so many ways, she has courageously battled over the years against agoraphobia and cancer. In a busy life they make the best of their leisure moments with several interests, including cricket, of course, gardening, painting, reading and listening to music.

SEVENTY YEARS ON

Work continued on the west-end of the Cathedral while the rest of the building was in constant use for services and celebrations. It had been expected that the money raised by the *Finish the Cathedral Appeal* would be sufficient to meet the total cost, but it became apparent that another huge sum was required.

RECONCILIATION

It was a challenge to the new Bishop when he arrived in the Diocese to support the new appeal and he did so with enthusiasm, believing that it was essential to complete the task begun in faith by an earlier generation. Dean Patey was delighted with the Bishop's ready response and justified the appeal, saying: "We are not just building the Cathedral for our own times, but for the enjoyment and inspiration of people a thousand years hence".[2]

The publicity to raise an additional half a million pounds was not helped when critics wrote to the press describing the Cathedral as "a twentieth century folly", or "a Liverpool tower-block" and "a nineteenth century ghost of medieval gothic". Even the *Financial Times* thought that the Cathedral "is likely to be a permanent headache for the Church of England authorities".[3] Nevertheless, while many felt that enough money had already been spent on the project and no more should be poured into it, some £250,000 was raised within four months and the Dean and Chapter were confident that the building of the Cathedral would be completed, prayers answered and faith rewarded.

Originally it was planned to hold the Dedication Service of the finished Cathedral in the presence of Her Majesty the Queen on Ascension Day 1978, seventy-four years after the laying of the foundation stone by her grandfather King George V, but because of the amount of work yet unfinished it was reluctantly decided to postpone the ceremony until a later date.

A splendid Dedication and Thanksgiving Service took place later on 25 October, the following year. which was imaginatively planned by the Chancellor, Canon Basil Naylor. It was centred around a theme suggested by the famous prayer of Sir Francis Drake, touching on *Beginning, Continuing* and *Finishing* a work to the glory of God. It was an impressive and joyful celebration in the presence of Queen Elizabeth II and a crowded congregation, with thousands witnessing the scene on television.

During the service Archbishop Worlock presented the Dean with a copy of the Jerusalem Bible, "as a token of our friendship and of the commitment we share to the Word of God". Archbishop Blanch returned to the Diocese for the great occasion and preached a forthright sermon on St Luke 19.39-40, reminding the congregation and TV audience that "the stones of this great cathedral from a quarry in Woolton have been shouting out since 1910, shouting about the High and Lofty One who inhabits eternity, but who is near to those who are of a humble and a contrite heart" He went on to apply the message, saying,, "If we as disciples of the Lord, keep on keeping quiet, these stones will shout aloud in succeeding generations as long as this nation remains a nation, and this city remains a city". In a final act, Bishop Sheppard dedicated the whole Cathedral to the glory of God and the service of Christ in the city and the world.

The Bishop has often described Liverpool Cathedral as "one of the great buildings of our century". It is a twentieth century masterpiece. Larger than either York Minister or Canterbury Cathedral it is the only Anglican Cathedral to be built in the Northern Province since the Reformation.

RECONCILIATION
BETTER TOGETHER
Within a few months of arriving in Liverpool the Bishop warmly welcomed the new Roman Catholic Archbishop, Derek Worlock, to the city. They were not complete strangers since they had both worked in the urban districts of London and occasionally met at meetings. Over the years the working relationship between the two of them developed into a close Christian fellowship. So close was the relationship that in the lovable humour of Liverpudlians they were affectionately known as "Fish and Chips" because they were always together and seldom out of the newspapers. The Bishop recalls how the friendship began with a call he made to the Archbishop's House on the day he moved in. He was the Archbishop's first visitor and together they talked and shared a bottle of wine which the Bishop had taken along. Two or three weeks later on Good Friday they again spoke together for half an hour over the phone simply sharing their faith "at the foot of the cross". From this small beginning a rich friendship developed and understanding began to mature between them so that it was natural they should meet regularly to discuss their work and pray together.

The bitter sectarianism, the prejudice and suspicion between Anglicans and Roman Catholics, which was a characteristic of religion in Liverpool in the past has now almost disappeared. Nevertheless, some Anglicans, feel that the Bishop has gone too far in cooperating so closely with the Roman Church. Undoubtedly the Second Vatican Council's more liberal stance has made it easier for the two Churches to draw closer together and generally at the end of the century people have a more tolerant attitude on matters of religion.

However, the Bishop and the Archbishop were both committed in their allegiance to their own Church, and recognised the fundamental differences between them, but both had a desire for a more peaceful co-existence between the two Communions. Both shared in services in each other's Cathedrals and churches, and one of the most inspiring events was the Covenant Service at Pentecost 1985, which began in the Metropolitan Cathedral with an inspiring sermon by Edward Patey, followed by a procession along Hope Street and concluded in the Anglican Cathedral. The Church leaders, representing the Anglicans, Roman Catholics and Free Churches on Merseyside, signed an Act of Covenant committing themselves to the service of Christ and his Gospel and to work together for closer unity. This has been taken up and developed into the signing of local Covenants in a number of areas.

It had been customary for representatives of the Free Churches to meet regularly for discussions with the Bishops, but it seemed to some that they had no official voice. To rectify this, the Bishop and the Archbishop were happy to invite the Free Churches to appoint an official spokesman and they chose the Rev. John Williamson, Moderator of the United Reformed Church, as their representative. Whenever called for in future, "the Liverpool Three" issued joint statements and took joint actions on important issues. When in 1985 Williamson moved on from Liverpool he was succeeded first by the Rev. Norwyn Denny and then by the Rev. Dr John Newton, both Chairmen of the Methodist District in Liverpool. The triple partnership has worked well for more than a decade and the Free Church contribution has added consider-

RECONCILIATION

able weight to their united initiatives. They have not been able to agree on every issue, but the bond of unity between the leaders has been strengthened and so also between the denominations. The enterprise has led over the years to the sharing of churches in the Diocese, Anglicans with Roman Catholics and Anglicans with Methodists.

Merseysiders are generally glad that the old sectarian hatred has died down, though there remains a Protestant concern in some quarters. Some members of the Orange Order interrupted Archbishop Worlock in his Lentern Address in Liverpool Parish Church by waving banners bearing Protestant slogans. A few days later they did the same thing when Dr Runcie, the Archbishop of Canterbury, began his sermon in the same church. Their unruly behaviour did the Protestant cause no good, and the Master of the Liverpool Orange Lodge immediately apologised for the disturbance caused by a militant few.

THE CENTENARY CELEBRATIONS

The celebrations marking one hundred years of God's blessings on the life and work of the Diocese began with a splendid Service of Dedication in the Cathedral on 14 November 1979, when Dr Cuthbert Bardsley, the Bishop of Coventry, preached the sermon in which he surveyed the progress of the Diocese over the years and raised the challenges of the future. Before the service ended, representatives of all the parishes presented to the Bishop their Centenary Thanksgiving Gifts and dedicated themselves to the service of God in the future.

In Centenary Year, both Michael Ramsey, the former Archbishop of Canterbury, and Stuart Blanch, the Archbishop of York, were invited back to Liverpool to preach at the commemorative services in the Cathedral. At the close of each service the whole congregation moved outside to sing the final hymn, symbolic of the good news for the world. Stuart Blanch also led the Lay Conference at Swanwick and later in the year he welcomed clergy and laity from the Diocese on pilgrimage to York. Another successful event, thoroughly enjoyed by young and old, clergy and laity, was the Family Festival Day at Haydock Race Course, a mixture of spirituality, worldly fun and human enjoyment. At the local level each deanery contributed to the celebrations by holding either a parish mission, a missionary event or even a concert.

As a permanent reminder of the Church's ministry on Merseyside over the past hundred years, the Diocese produced a very attractive, illustrated brochure, *Portrait of a Diocese, 1880-1980*, with a foreword by the Bishop. The booklet has some excellent photographs of past and present leaders in the Diocese with a brief resumé of their contributions to the life of the Church.

THE TOXTETH RIOTS

The serious disturbances which broke out in Toxteth on a warm evening in July 1981 were suddenly ignited when a black youth was arrested on suspicion of taking a motorcycle without consent. The incident led to a violent confrontation between

RECONCILIATION

hundreds of black youths and the police in riot gear. For several nights there was rioting, petrol bombing and wholesale destruction of property. Miraculously, a Bible College, Synagogue and Anglo-Catholic Church in the centre of the rioting, all escaped damage.

The Bishop was away on study leave when the troubles started and on hearing how the situation had developed decided to return to Liverpool. The riots lasted for several weeks and probably had several causes: drugs, unemployment, frustration, anti-police attitudes and even the hot, sultry weather.

It was to the Bishop and the Archbishop that the older generation of Toxteth turned to for help in their time of need. They made themselves available and in the following days they were often seen in the streets of the stricken neighbourhood talking with people in an effort to defuse the inflammatory situation and eventually bring about reconciliation between the warring parties. The problem, of course, was too big for them to solve, but behind the scenes they acted as "go-betweens" and managed to bring the opposing sides together for talks. A major step forward was the Chief Constable's invitation to the Bishops to chair a meeting of the Police Committee to promote peace and reconciliation within the community. This led eventually to setting up the successful "community policing" in the area. The Bishops went on to urge the Government to appoint a Minister for Merseyside, who would come to the city and listen to the Liverpudlian point of view and take action to improve the deprived areas.

THE PAPAL VISIT

One of the highlights of the decade for many on Merseyside was the visit to Liverpool in May 1982 of Pope John Paul II. The primary purpose of his visit was to celebrate Mass in the new Metropolitan Cathedral and since Catholics and Anglicans had begun to work closer together in recent years it seemed appropriate to include in the itinerary a visit to the Anglican Cathedral.

After celebrating Mass on the fifteenth anniversary of the consecration of the Cathedral of Christ the King, the Pope, accompanied by Archbishop Worlock, was driven in the famous Popemobile to the Anglican Cathedral, where they received a tremendous welcome from the waiting crowd. A small group of demonstrators protested by raising aloft copies of the Bible and the Union Jack, but they were largely ignored by the crowds. Pope John was warmly welcomed at the entrance of the Cathedral by the Dean and the Bishops of Liverpool and Warrington. The congregation filling every available space in the nave, broke with tradition and began clapping and cheering in appreciation when the Pope entered. So loud was the spontaneous hand-clapping that it almost drowned out the the organ and the processional hymn.

In the ecumenical service which followed, the Pope exchanged the kiss of peace, led the congregation in the Lord's Prayer and at the close gave his Papal blessing, "Christ is our peace, He has reconciled us to God in one body by the Cross. We meet in his name and share his peace". It was an impressive and memorable service.

RECONCILIATION

Leaving the Cathedral the Pope travelled the whole length of Hope Street, back to the Metropolitan Cathedral, between cheering crowds. Some find rich symbolism in the fact that Hope Street links the two Cathedrals like a ribbon drawing them closer together.

On reflection, Bishop David commented after the event: "The Pope's visit was an uplift, a support and an encouragement to the very real partnership between Anglicans and Catholics that is developing here. I think Liverpool will be a better place for his having been here".[4]

There was genuine sorrow on Merseyside in February 1996 when it was announced that Archbishop Derek Warlock had died after suffering from lung cancer. On his translation to the Archdiocese he set about refurbishing church structures and reviving spiritual life in his Communion. He sponsored the Liverpool Pastoral Congress in 1980 and was responsible for persuading the Pope to include the Anglican Cathedral in his visit to Liverpool.

In July the Archdiocese welcomed Patrick Kelly, the Bishop of Salford, Derek Warlock's successor, when he was installed in the Metropolitan Cathedral. He is a dogmatic theologian with a liberal and ecumenical outlook and it is hoped that the close relations which have developed between the Churches will continue.

BIAS TO THE POOR

David Sheppard had spent eighteen years in the working-class boroughs of south and east London before moving up to Liverpool. In his ministry he had become acutely aware of the misery caused by poverty, unemployment and deprivation, and when he came to Liverpool he found the same economic and social conditions. He was burdened by the Church's apparent lack of concern for the poor and under privileged and believed that Christians are called to identify with the disadvantaged and stand alongside the poor and needy. David Sheppard was the obvious man in 1991 to take over the Chairmanship of the General Synod Board of Social Responsibilities and was a great influence on many of its future decisions relating to urban and social deprivation. He took time off from the Diocese in 1981 for prayer and study and two years later published his book *Bias to the Poor*. It is a challenge to the whole Church to have a concern for the oppressed and destitute and to be involved in relieving the injustices and prejudices in society which "imprison the spirit". Much of the material in the book arose out of personal episodes in the Diocese which engaged the Bishop.

When, for instance, it was mooted that Dunlop's, a major firm on Merseyside, which for generations had given regular employment to thousands of Liverpudlians, was about to close with the loss of more than five thousand jobs, the shop stewards appealed to Sheppard and Worlock for their support to keep the factory open. The two Bishops willingly headed the march of the workers through the streets of the city to the traditional meeting place at the Pier Head. The working classes generously applauded their stand with them and the readiness of the Churches to identify with their cause.

RECONCILIATION

The Bishop's book, *Bias to the Poor* received mixed reviews and was savaged in some quarters. Some of his critics felt that he had got his priorities wrong and had now adopted a liberal theology and a social gospel. But the Bishop stood his ground, maintaining that the gospel of reconciliation is concerned not only with uniting God and man but also man with man. "When I was ordained", he confessed, "I believed that the gospel was about changing individuals from inside out....At no time have I moved away from that belief that Christ changes individuals. But I came to see that Christians must be concerned with something else too: we are called to change the course of events, as far as that lies within our power."[5] The Bishop's crusade for social justice has been taken up by several churches in the Diocese and some clergy have taken courses in counselling and social work to fit them for this specialised ministry. The Church, in general, is now beginning to show a genuine and practical concern for one-parent families, the long-term unemployed and those caught in the poverty trap. Where Community churches have been opened they meet a need in welcoming in the unemployed, young families and pensioners for games, handicrafts and refreshments.

The untiring efforts of Bishop David and Archbishop Derek on behalf of the disadvantaged in society have been widely recognised and to their great surprise and the joy of many the City Fathers in 1995 conferred the Freedom of the City on the Bishops at a magnificent ceremony in St George's Hall.

DERRICK WALTERS

On the retirement of Edward Patey from the Deanery in 1982 the Crown appointed Derrick Walters, Canon Residentiary and Treasurer of Sarum Cathedral as the new Dean of England's largest Cathedral. He was installed on the 14th January 1983 by Eric Corbett, the Canon Treasurer. In his first sermon in the Cathedral the Dean emphasised the importance and relevance of Cathedrals in the modern world as an integral part of the Christian mission and a constant reminder that man is a moral and spiritual being with responsibilities toward both God and his fellow-man. Under the Dean's leadership the daily acts of choral praise and worship and the great festival services at Christmas, Easter and Pentecost continue to uplift the congregation and resound to the glory of God.

Not long after taking up residence in the Deanery, the Dean began seriously to consider to what use the sloping land on the west side of the Cathedral could be put. He has been the inspiration and driving force behind the Rosemary Project, which included the creation of Cathedral College, an estate of attractive buildings, adjacent to the Cathedral, providing modern, comfortable accommodation for students studying in the city, together with circular courts of attractive private residences. The initiative has also contributed to urban regeneration in the creation of the new Liverpool Women's Hospital and a development by the Local Housing Association on derelict land a short distance away. The project has brought the Cathedral and the City closer together. Another of his worthwhile developments within the Cathedral is the Visitors Centre and the Refectory, which is said to be "the most beautiful cafe

RECONCILIATION

in the country" and is a welcome refreshment stop for visitors. It also makes a significant contribution, along with the Bookshop, to the annual income of the Cathedral. The Dean is forward looking and, following a recent comprehensive review of the work of the Cathedral, is anxious to improve the already high standards of worship, management and voluntary service, which the Cathedral Chapter contributes to the mission of the Church.

THE DIOCESAN SYNOD

The Synod has debated several important issues in recent years and reports have been passed on to the Deanery Synods at local level for information and further discussion. Among the topics on the agenda have been the new Baptism Service, Woman Priests, Diocesan Reorganisation and most recently Clergy Conditions of Service. At present when the clergy are inducted and instituted into a benefice they enjoy the security of the freehold for as long as they they wish to remain in the incumbency. The problem is that very occasionally a clergyman may stay too long in a parish, perhaps neglect his pastoral work or even be a misfit and no one has the authority to move him on. The parson's freehold has always been considered a valuable asset in the ministry of the Church of England and beneficed clergy are very anxious not to lose this right. They value their independence and vigorously defend the status quo, and so concerned are some clergy that they have taken the unusual step of joining a trade union to protect their interests. A Steering Group was set up in the Diocese to examine the whole matter and to present the case for and against change. Deaneries have had the opportunity to discuss and vote on the matter and when the subject came before the Diocesan Synod the members were obviously influenced by the deanery decisions and voted by a narrow majority in favour of qualified changes, together with a system devised to allow the removal of inefficient clergy.

THE LIVE WIRE

For many years the Diocesan Leaflet with recent news about the Church in the Diocese was displayed on a table at the back of churches for parishioners to pick up or it was slipped inside the Parish Magazine awaiting delivery. The leaflet was inexpensive and had a wide circulation but it was old fashioned in format. It ceased publication in 1984 when the Diocese produced a new and modern publication: an eight-page tabloid newspaper with articles, snippets and photographs of interest to church folk. Canon Dick Williams was the inspiration behind the new venture and became its first editor. Since its small beginning *The Livewire* went on from strength to strength and at one time the free paper had a circulation of 57,000 copies, but in 1988 reached a crisis point when the Diocese had to make the decision either to make a small charge for the paper or cease publication. It is a valuable means of communication and its life was prolonged and eight years on it is eagerly awaited each month by appreciative readers. From the first issue, readers have been drawn to read on by some captivating head-line or caption such as *Mersey Miracle*, celebrating the growth of Christian unity in the Diocese or *Easter Hope and Healing*, fol-

79

RECONCILIATION

lowing the 1989 tragedy at Hillsborough. A popular series has been the *Bishop Writes* on some relevant and challenging theme and *Parish Profile*, focussing on the history and work of individual parishes in the Diocese.

RURAL MINISTRY

The report of the Archbishop's Commission on Rural Areas, *Faith in the Countryside* was recently published and has been carefully studied in the Diocese. Liverpool is largely an industrial Diocese but outside the urban areas there are wide expanses of agricultural land and a fair proportion of the Diocesan clergy minister in rural parishes. Country parishes arc often served by older clergy and it is sometimes overlooked that they often feel isolated and deprived because of a lack of resources in a small rural community. The Diocese initiated a pilot study of rural deprivation in the Burscough area, which then led on to a full scale study of the problem throughout the Diocese. The findings confirmed that rural parishes face many problems, such as a lack of amenities, few shops, infrequent public transport and a shortage of low rent housing for the local people. The clergy generally find that they have more than one parish to look after, often without the assistance of trained laity generally available in urban priority areas.

The Report helps to raise the profile of the rural ministry in the Diocese and shows a need to develop patterns of worship, evangelism and pastoral ministry appropriate to the countryside. A particular problem facing country parishes is the demand to meet the rising Diocesan Quota where congregations are small. The Rural Forum set up to consider countryside issues and report back to the Bishop's Council is a useful sounding-board. A recent initiative taken by the Board of Ministry is to offer further training to those drawn to rural ministry together with refresher courses for those already serving in rural parishes.

THE DECADE OF EVANGELISM

The Anglican Bishops attending the Lamberth Conference in 1988 challenged the Church to turn its attention from Maintenance to Mission and to unite with other Churches in "renewed and united emphasis in making Christ known to the people of the world". The Decade of Evangelism was officially launched in 1990 and to give an imputus to the project the Archbishops a couple of years later commissioned *Springboard,* a team of evangelists to work within the dioceses leading parish and deanery missions, visiting schools and colleges and holding conferences for training clergy and laity.

The Decade of Evangelism began in Liverpool Diocese with a Pastoral Letter from the Bishop requesting every parish to prayerfully consider and define its pastoral aims and intentions till the close of the century. These "Intentions for the Decade" from 209 parishes were presented to the Bishop at a Decade Service in the Cathedral in September 1992, and the Bishop responded by commissioning the parishes to carry out their agendas with God's blessing.

The Decade Support Group, chaired by the Bishop of Warrington, has given

RECONCILIATION

invaluable help to parishes from the beginning of the project, arranging day conferences on *The Logic of Evangelism* and another on *Give a Good Account of Your
Faith – Today!* and more recently on *Growing Into Faith* and three aspects of
Evangelism and Worship. These training sessions have been well attended and
proved challenging and instructive. In addition to the teaching and training sessions
the Support Group, now succeeded by the Laity Training Team has made available
a wealth of resource material to help Christians the better "to know the faith, to live
the faith and to share the faith".

Dr. George Carey, the Archbishop of Canterbury, spent four days in the Diocese
in 1993, especially to learn what impact the Decade was having on the parishes. He
was greatly impressed by the various initiatives being undertaken and to learn that
the Diocese intended to make three part-time appointments, a Diocesan Evangelist,
and Adviser in Evangelism and a Children's Evangelist.

One notable effort in the Decade was the coming together of some forty churches in a united witness in the town-centre of St. Helens. A marquee was set up in the
busy precinct and for a whole week Christians shared their faith in Christ with
passers-by and interested shoppers. "The Liverpool Three" also added their voices
at the end of the week. The initiative demonstrated that Christians are united and
attempted to show that the gospel is relevant for modern man.

During May 1996, the *Springboard* team led by Bishop Michael Marshall and
Canon Michael Green, conducted the Liverpool Training School in various centres
of the Diocese with a Lay Training Day at St. Joseph's College, Upholland attended
by more than four hundred delegates. The team inspired and challenged both clergy
and laity by their enthusiasm, ideas and workshops on various topics.

The Decade is now half way through. To some it appears to have run out of steam,
but on a closer examination there are unmistakable signs of life. It was never intended to hold some great one-off event, but rather a long-term outreach taking on a variety of forms. Some parish ventures in mission have been successful while others
have not worked so well. Aware of this, Bishop David and Bishop Michael have
been making a series of deanery visits encouraging parishes to fulfil their Decade
"intentions", to make more use of the Diocesan missioners and available resources
and to be more ecumenical in outlook. It is imperative that Christians start to put
more effort into the Decade by being more prayerful, more expectant and more
effective in their witness. The Church in the Diocese has a God-given mission to
make known the good news of Jesus Christ in the power of the Spirit so that people
will come to trust in him as Saviour and Lord and then to build them up in the
Christian faith within the Christian fellowship.

PARTNERS IN MISSION

In 1978 when the Bishops from the whole of the Anglican Communion were in
England for the Lambeth Conference the Diocese invited several Bishops from overseas to visit Liverpool to speak about the Church in their dioceses. The visit developed into a partnership between the Church in this Diocese and the Church in Africa,

RECONCILIATION

Canada and South America. The partnership was strengthened by Bill Flagg, an Assistant Bishop in the Diocese at the time, who had been a missionary in South America and served as a Bishop in Peru. In 1980 Colin Bazley, formerly incumbent of St Leonard's, Bootle, and now Bishop in Chile and Presiding Bishop of the Sourthern Cone of America, presented Bishop David with a chalice and paton made of Chilean copper on behalf of the Anglican Church in South America. From time to time on missionary occasions the communion vessels are used by the clergy in the Diocese. The bonds of fellowship with the Church overseas have grown considerably stronger over the years and the Diocese now has close ties with the Church in Europe, Canada, the United States, Australia and New Zealand, South America, Africa, Pakistan, Bangladesh, the Middle East and South East Asia.

In 1983 the Diocese of Akure was created out of the larger Diocese of Ondo in Nigeria. The Church in this Diocese soon established a close relationship with the new Diocese in West Africa, and this has led to links being forged between some parishes and schools in the twinned Dioceses together with plans for an interchange of young people and long stay visits by clergy from Nigeria. In September 1995 Bishop Emmanuel and his wife visited the Diocese for a short time and the following year Archdeacon Justus Olugasa and his wife spent a year in the parish of St Mark's, Kirkby. Unfortunately the political situation in Nigeria under a military regime has meant the postponement of these visits and drawn attention to the need for urgent prayer for the Church in Nigeria.

MICHAEL HENSALL

The Bishop and the Diocese have been enthusiastically supported by Michael Henshall, the Bishop of Warrington, since 1976. He was the vicar of St George's, Altrincham and a canon of Chester Cathedral when Bishop David invited him to join him in Liverpool. Belonging to the High Church wing of the Church, Bishop Michael found no difficulty in working amicably alongside Bishop David and together over the years they have maintained a perfect balance in episcopal partnership. Michael has been a popular Bishop and his sermons, especially those addressed to Men, will long be remembered. In addition to fulfiling the usual episcopal duties he has undertaken numerous responsibilities in the Diocese, including in recent times the chairmanship of the Pastoral Committee, the Decade of Evangelism Support Group and an Ecumenical Working Party investigating the problems of unemployment, low pay and social security benefits. He has also taken a special interest in the establishment of the Merseyside and Regions Churches Ecumenical Assembly and the training of ordinands through the North West Ordination Course. It was a special joy recently for Michael, the son of a priest, to see his own son ordained in the Diocese of Newcastle. When he retires with his wife Steve to Scarborough after serving the Diocese for twenty years, he will be followed by John Packer, the Archdeacon of West Cumberland since 1991, who will be consecrated the Bishop of Warrington in November 1996.

RECONCILIATION

CLERGY APPRAISAL

One of the Bishop's major concerns when he came to the Diocese was to ascertain how efficient and effective was the parochial ministry. It was recognised that there were great demands on a clergyman's time and energy and a need to sit back and quietly review from time to time what really has been achieved in the parish over the past year. On the Bishop's recommendation the Diocese set up in 1976 the Diocesan Joint Work Consultation, the first such scheme in the Church of England. On a voluntary and confidential basis it was proposed that the parochial clergy should meet annually with senior clergy; curates with vicars, vicars with area-deans and even bishops with bishops, to assess the aims and achievements of their ministry. It was not intended to be an imposition from the top. The project had some problems to overcome in the beginning and in practice has been modified and improved.

Again, on the Bishop's initiative a working party was established to consider the establishment of a Self-Appraisal Scheme in addition to a review of their work through the Joint Work Consultation. The Working Party discussed all the aspects of the scheme and the Liverpool Self-Assessment Scheme was launched in 1989 after it had won the whole-hearted approval of the Deanery Chapters. The scheme has a mandatory element and demands of the clergy a self-assessment every three years. Clergy meet with their Area Dean or other approved Appraiser, who has received some training in interviewing and management skills and together they discuss all aspects of their ministry in the light of their ordination vows. A report of the Appraisal is then submitted to the Bishop, which keeps him in touch with his clergy and informed of what is happening in the parishes. As a follow-up, the Bishop may suggest some clergy taking in-service courses and so developing their talents. The Scheme is intended to benefit both clergy and parishes and no doubt parishioners will] be delighted if the Appraisal helps to produce a more earnest and caring ministry.

THE DIOCESE TODAY

In the past twenty or thirty years there have been many dramatic changes in the Church of England which have significantly affected every Diocese.

Vicars used to live in large, cold Victorian vicarages, but most of these have been sold and the vicar and his family now reside in a modern, centrally heated home with a small, pleasant garden.

The vicar was frequently seen visiting or cycling around his parish, but now he usually passes by in the parish car. He is rarely recognised in the street as a clergyman since he prefers not to wear a "dog-collar", except perhaps on Sundays.

Until very recent times clergy did not have the advantage of modern technology but now parishes are adopting modern business practices and appointing personal secretaries and equipping the parish office with computers, colour printers and answering machines.

The clergy were often called on by a parishioner in trouble or seeking advice, but counselling now seems to have been taken over to a large extent by the doctor, the social services and the solicitor.

RECONCILIATION

The parish church used to be left open for anyone who wished to call in for quiet and prayer. but now because of fear of thefts, vandalism and rising insurance the doors are often locked except during service time.

Years ago clergy were left to get on with the work in the parish and sometimes felt isolated though they could call on the rural-dean or the Bishop for advice when they had a particular problem, but now parishes, especially in urban areas, are often linked together in team ministries and there is a greater sharing of the ministry.

In the past when a clergyman wished to move to another parish he spoke to his Bishop or other patron and awaited in prayer an invitation to fill a vacancy. Now vacancies are often advertised in the Church press and clergy send in an application together with the usual curriculum vitae.

At one time it was most unusual for a clergyman's wife to go out to work and she was expected to devote much of her time to the parish and organise the Womens' Meeting and run the Mothers' Union, but now many clergy wives were engaged in professions before marriage and choose to continue in full or part-time employment afterwards.

The Alternative Service Book has now virtually replaced the Book of Common Prayer in the majority of churches. The General Synod introduced the revised prayer book in 1980 and it has been generally welcomed by clergy and laity in the Diocese. It was hoped that the new forms of service, with later editions of the main services published in booklet form, together with modern versions of the Bible, contemporary prayers and modern hymns with bright tunes, would persuade lapsed members to return to church and attract new-comers, but attendances continue to decline. It was a mistake to suppose that modernising the services alone would bring people in. On the contrary, the spontaneity and informality introduced into the services as churches fashion their own patterns of worship, have been divisive and led to many loyal Anglicans continuing to believe but ceasing to belong. However, some churches with contemporary services have been encouraged, particularly by the number of young couples with families attending.

The outpouring of the Spirit on some parts of the Church in recent times and the trend to modernise worship has changed the face of the Church of England in several ways. Chancels have been opened up in some churches and the communion table brought down into the nave, the solid oak pews have been removed and semi-circles of chairs have taken their place; the traditional order of worship has gone and the laity have a more active role, participating fully to the accompaniment of guitars, keyboards and percussion instruments. Often in charismatic churches the laity are enthusiastic and ready to use their gifts in a variety of ways. The changes have been upsetting and painful to some congregations, who felt a loss of transcendence, holiness and reverence in worship. Nevertheless, these churches have been the fastest growing in recent time and those in the Diocese which have experienced renewal have been singularly blessed.

The debate over the ordination of women has also divided the Church, but in Liverpool the Diocese has generally been in favour and the transition has been car-

RECONCILIATION

ried through smoothly with several women priests working happily in parishes, hospitals, schools and colleges. The way has been opened for women priests to be appointed archdeacons, deans and provosts and in Liverpool the first woman priest has been appointed an Area Dean.

It is known that several Bishops are due to retire and it is expected that some younger Bishops will be leading the Church into the twenty-first century. It is believed in some quarters that Bishop David may be retiring in the not distant future after a long and successful episcopate, and then church folk in the Diocese will again be wondering, " Who is going to be the next Bishop?"

In its short history the Diocese has made remarkable progress in spite of many difficulties and the ministry and mission of the Church has been richly blessed down the years. As the new Millennium draws near the Church will be faced with many new challenges, but the Diocese appears to be in good heart and ready to go forward with confidence in the strength of the Lord, The evidence of history clearly shows that Liverpool Diocese is *Not a Dead See.*

Notes

Chapter 1 — A New Diocese

1   *Liverpool Daily Post*, 9 January 1875.
2   A. Hume, *A Detailed Account of how Liverpool became a Diocese*, 1881, p.18.
3   W. Jacobson, Visitation Charge 1877.
4   J. C. Ryle, Primary Visitation Charge 1881.
5   The Bishopric Committee Subscription List.

Chapter 2 — Foundation

1   Peter Toon, ed., *J. C. Ryle A Self-Portrait*, 1974, p.40.
2   Ibid.
3   Ibid., p.53.
4   Ibid., p.67.
5   J. C. Ryle, Triennial Visitation Charge, 1893.
6   *Liverpool Courier*, 10 March 1900.
7   J. C. Ryle, Diocesan Conference, 1887.
8   Q. Hughes, Seaport Architecture and Townscape in Liverpool, 1964, p.113.
9   O. R. Clarke, "The First Bishop of Liverpool", in *The Churchman*, vol. LXIX, 1955, p.226.
10 J. C. Ryle, Address on "The Laity", Hull Congress Report, 1890.
11 *The Church of England Year Book*, 1885, p. xviii.
12 M. C. Church, *Life and Letters of Dean Church*, 1894, p.336.
13 Ibid., p.151.
14 J. C. Ryle, *Knots Untied*, 1874, p.505.
15 J. C. Ryle, *Principles for Churchmen*, 1884, pp.418-419.
16 Ibid., p.419.
17 R. Hobson, *What Hath God Wrought*, 1903, p.293.

Chapter 3 — Consolidation

1   J. B. Lancelot, *Francis James Chavasse*, p.143.
2   J. B. Lancelot, "Bishop Chavasse, 1846-1928", in *Great Christians*, ed, F. S. Forman, 1933., p.104.
3   Ibid., p.102.
4   Ibid., p.101.
5   J. B. Lancelot, *Francis James Chavasse*, p.175.
6   Peter Kennerley, *The Building of Liverpool Cathedral*, 1991, p.15.
7   Ibid., p.16.
8   Vere E. Cotton, "The Building of Liverpool Cathedral" in *The Liverpool Review*, vol, V, July 1930, p.300.
9   *The Times*, 11 October 1904.
10 J. B. Lancelot, in *Great Christians*, p.83.
11 J. B, Lancelot, *Francis James Chavasse*, p.199 footnote.
12 J. Cottrell, *How Southport got its Churches*, p. 1
13 F. A. Bailey, *History of Southport*, 1955, p.122 .
14 J. B. Lancelot, Ibid., p.227.
15 J. B. Lancelot in *Great Christians*, p.109.
16 J, B. Lancelot, *Francis James Chavasse*, p.258.
17 Op.cit., p.279.
18 Ibid, p.285.

Chapter 4 — Organisation
1   Peter Kennerley, *The Building of Liverpool Cathedral*, 1991, pp.74-75.
2   *The Manchester Guardian*, 21 July 1924.
3   *The Liverpool Review*, vol. V, July 1930, p.237.
4   John. S. Peart-Binns, "Albert Augustus David" in *Four Bishops of Liverpool*, 1985, p. 40.
5   Joe Riley, *Today's Cathedral*, 1978, p.105.
6   John. S. Peart-Binns, Ibid., p.51.
7   Ibid., p.46.

Chapter 5 — Mission
1   Bill Bailey, "Clifford Arthur Martin", in *Four Bishops of Liverpool*, p.63.
2   Liverpool Daily Post, 11 June 1955.
3   Joe Riley, *Today's Cathedral*, p.96.
4   Bill Bailey, Ibid., p.65.

Chapter 6 — Edification
1   *The Times*, 16 July 1994.
2   Ibid.
3   Joe Riley, Ibid., p.7.
4   Edward H. Patey, *My Liverpool Life*, p.9.
5   Ibid, p.14.
6   Ibid, p.10.
7   *Diocesan News*, May 1969.
8   *The Times*, Ibid.

Chapter 7 — Reconciliation
1   Christopher Martin Jenkins, *The Complete Who's Who of Test Cricket*, 1987, p.138.
2   Edward H. Patey, *My Liverpool Life*, 1983, p.20.
3   Ibid, p. 32.
4   *The Times*, 31 May 1982.
5   David Sheppard and Derek Worlock, *Better Together*, 1998, p.28.